So Great
A Salvation

Chip & Elizabeth,

God is always good and
always faithful to His Word.

I love you!

II Corinthians 3:18

Douglas

So Great A Salvation

*Moving From Good to Great
in Your Relationship with the Father*

by

Douglas Crumbly

Connecting people to God.

iconnect publications
324 Mathis Dr
Rome GA 30165
706.234.4923

So Great a Salvation

ISBN: 0-9779791-0-5

Published by iconnect publications
324 Mathis Dr
Rome GA 30165
United States of America

Art Direction: Stephen Carswell, Terri Beth Carswell

Editors: Shelly Burkhalter, Sandra Broome

Printed in the United States of America by PrintWorks. www.goprintworks.com

*"The peace we crave, the prosperity we desire, the deliverance we need"
- it is all in Christ - everything we need to create a little bit of Heaven
here on Earth. Jesus did come to make us happy, and Pastor Douglas
Crumbly in his timely book, So Great A Salvation, establishes that
truth from the Word of God. Then he goes one step better and tells us
how to get there. I love books that teach me the truth and then show
me how to live it. I recommend you allow this book to do the same for
you and help you create your own bit of Heaven here on Earth.*

- Jerry Savelle
  Jerry Savelle Ministries
  Crowley, Texas

*Douglas Crumbly is a happy man and, as a personal friend of his, I
know this is true. In his new book, Douglas tells you how you can
learn to walk in the true happiness and joy of the salvation Jesus has
so freely given us. Too many Christians live oppressed and defeated
lives, and I believe this book will teach you how to experience the life
in Christ you have always desired.*

- Terry Nance
  Author of *God's Armorbearer*

*Finally someone simplistically explains the great love and work of
Jesus Christ. Douglas Crumbly transparently shares his wonderful
relationship with God and teaches us how to enjoy what Jesus Christ
has done. So Great a Salvation should be read by anyone who calls
himself a Christian. I thank God for this book. It will change your life!*

- Dr. Robert Watkins
  Founder and President, Kings-Priests International
  Author of *How to Hear from God*

Pastor Douglas Crumbly has given to us a crystal clear message of the wonderful realities of our redemption in Christ and provided guideposts for our journey of growth in them. His practical, down to earth style communicates these realities in simple clarity. The truths shared in this book bring us back to the work of the cross in the life of the believer and the glorious life it produces. Pastor Crumbly reminds mature believers of their position and possessions in Christ and the simple acts of faith that made them so real in their lives. For new believers, he unfolds the wonderful life that is now theirs in Christ and lays out a simple roadmap to help them in their journey of growth.

- Dr. Steve Vickers
  President, Harvest Churches International
  Pastor emeritus, Christian Life Church
  Montgomery, Alabama

Pastor Douglas Crumbly teaches the truths of the Christian walk with simplicity making the message of his book practical to those who read it. He challenges Christians to live victoriously, to rejoice, and to enjoy this great salvation.

- Miguel and Maria Paula Arrazola
  Pastors of River of Life Church in Cartegena, Colombia
  Regional Directors, CEBCO

So many believers in Christ never receive their inheritance in Christ. To receive an inheritance, one must understand that it exists and actuate it. In this valuable book, So Great A Salvation, Pastor Douglas Crumbly imparts to the reader a clear understanding of the riches we have been given through Christ's sacrificial death and how to actuate the inheritance for our lives. Read every detail of the will Christ left for you, and work to receive the abundantly rich life He died to provide.

- Dr. Dean R. Radtke, Founder & CEO
  The Institute of Ministry Management and Leadership

This book is dedicated to all the men and women
who have taught me the truth of God's Word and helped
me to have a greater appreciation for being saved.

I also dedicate this book to my wife, Debbie,
for your encouragement and consistency
in drawing out the best in me.

So GREAT A Salvation

*Moving from Good to Great
in your Relationship with the Father*

Table of Contents

Introduction ....*xiii*

Acknowledgement ....*xvii*

Chapter 1 ....*EXceed* *1*

Chapter 2 ....*EXonerate* *9*

Chapter 3 ....*EXpel* *21*

Chapter 4 ....*EXchange* *31*

Chapter 5 ....*EXtravagant* *45*

Chapter 6 ....*EXhibit* *53*

Chapter 7 ....*EXcel* *65*

Chapter 8 ....*EXtol* *73*

Chapter 9 ....*EXalt* *81*

Chapter 10 ....*EXperience* *91*

Chapter 11 ....*EXecute* *105*

Notes *115*

Introduction

From my earliest memories of being saved I knew there had to be more than what I was exposed to. I knew I was going to go to Heaven, but something inside of me was constantly drawing me to the understanding that there had to be more to salvation than just getting there. That's what this book is about. I felt compelled to write a book that would help you to have a better understanding of who the Word says you are, now that you are in Christ, and what Jesus, through the Holy Spirit, is doing in you. It is vital to your Christianity to have an understanding of what these truths are and how they apply to your life.

When I gave my life to Jesus years ago, it was because I was afraid of ending up in Hell. I remember the preaching on how hot Hell is and how the worms never die. I remember the fear I felt when I watched the movie, *The Burning Hell*. I was so convicted of my sin and so terrified of eternal damnation that I got saved as soon as I could. I understood that doing so meant that Jesus would come into my heart and life. I knew in a sense that I was giving my life to Him, but I had no idea what this salvation experience really meant. I knew for certain that I was saved from Hell, which was enough at that moment. But over the years, I would struggle with issues in my life - circumstances, broken relationships, difficult and painful times - and I needed to have real answers to the questions that plagued me. I was searching like many of you. I desperately wanted to know the truth about God. Did He love me? Was He good? Was He concerned about my life and about my future? Was He aware of the pain I was feeling? Would He really love me enough to move in my life? At that time, you must understand that I was not sure that God would even hear me much less answer me. And I was convinced that if He did answer, He would probably say no because I knew I wasn't deserving of anything good.

I had been beaten down by life and had a negative view of everything around me including God. But in the midst of all of that, amazingly, there was hope that maybe God wanted to help me, maybe He wanted to rescue me and deliver me. So I searched for answers. I talked to Christian leaders that I respected. I read and studied the Bible. This book is a result of my pursuit of God. It is a product of the process God has taken me through and the wisdom I have gained by seeking Him and seeking to know His ways. Jesus told us in Matthew 11:29 to learn from Him. That is what I have purposed to do for the last twenty years or so.

Hebrews 2:3 says, "How shall we escape if we neglect so great a salvation?" Being saved from Hell is absolutely wonderful and beyond what my words could express, but I am thankful that as I escaped the grip of Hell, I was embraced by a loving Heavenly Father who gave me everything I would need to navigate the course of life. He gave me Himself through His Word, His Spirit, His name, His blood, and His church. All of these are necessary and all are for my good. And because of these gifts, I will never be the same again. My salvation began in a moment, but what a life changing moment it was. A way was made and a door was opened into an abundant life that Jesus came to give me. It was so great a salvation that I cannot fully explain it within these pages, but it is my prayer that what I do share will change your thinking, your words, your actions, and ultimately your life.

It is my desire that as you read this book, you will grow in your understanding of how God loves you with all of the love He can give, and not only that, but that you will have a greater appreciation for what He has done for you. It is only then that you will move from having a good relationship with your Father to a great one and that you will fully experience His GREAT SALVATION.

Acknowledgement

I want to personally thank all of the people who helped me with this book. Without you, this would have only been a dream. But now, because of your hard work and long hours, this dream has been birthed into a book that will help many. Sandra Broome, for your encouraging words and critical eye. Stephen and Terri Beth Carswell, for your creativity and diligence. Mike Robinson and PrintWorks, for your excellence in printing. I *especially* want to thank Shelly Burkhalter for all the hard work you did in editing and reviewing late into the night, re-reading the text dozens of times, and the supreme excellence you've shown in helping me to take this book from my heart to the printed page. You all are a blessing.

— *Douglas Crumbly*

EXCEED

ex-ceed \ik-'sēd\ *1: to extend outside of*
2: to be greater than or superior to : SURPASS
3: to go beyond a limit set by

Chapter 1

———————•———————

Exceeding The Norm

———————•———————

I am a happy man. This may seem to be an odd way to begin a book, but I truly am. Believe me when I tell you this, I have had as many opportunities to be unhappy as the next man. It's just that I am enjoying being saved. I want you to enjoy it as well. Too many believers are going through life with little or no understanding about the joy of salvation, much less how to appropriate that joy in times of crisis. We have become content with putting up with life instead of really living it the way Jesus intended. We know internet, downloads, and instant messaging. PDA's, cell phones, and GPS are as common as candy. Medical advances are hard to keep up with, and the increase of knowledge has become simply mind-boggling. Information at our finger tips and hundreds of sure fire ways to make our life easier and less complicated have not made us any happier. The truth be known, they probably have made us more unhappy. When will we understand that things, no matter how shiny and fast, will never fill the void we all have?

Consider the following quote from the Toronto Star on December 29, 2003:

> *"The World Values Survey, an inter-university study, recently reported that Nigerians are the happiest people in the world. The survey ranks only some 20 of 62 countries surveyed. Canada's ranking isn't listed but it's above the United States (16th) and Britain (24th) while Russians are ranked the unhappiest. The survey, which has studied happiness since 1945, finds it has not increased in Europe and North America even though the societies have become wealthier. The desire for material goods, it concludes, is 'a happiness suppressant'."* [1]

I can really say that it is because of my salvation that I am happy. I know, I know, we have all been told that Jesus did not come to make us happy, but holy. This usually is spoken by an unhappy person I might add, for Jesus did come to make us happy. I want to reiterate this because a lot of people who say they are Christians are not happy. I meet them all of the time. They go to church, tithe, and volunteer, yet do not enjoy being saved. Although it is true that becoming a believer does not make us immune to life's difficulties, salvation does give us an advantage. Knowledge of this advantage is the thing that makes us happy. And it should. Believers struggle with the same issues and problems that non-believers do. Without a good understanding of what has taken place when they received Jesus, they will continue to make the same decisions and draw the same conclusions as they did before and ultimately get the same results. Doing so will cause them to continue to live in a pit of despair, lacking true happiness.

Actually, the Bible is full of scriptures that teach us that God is the source of true happiness, and until we learn to look to Him, we will never experience happiness the way it was meant to be experienced. Let's look at three different scripture references that bring this truth home.

Happy is he who has the God of Jacob for his help, whose hope is in the Lord his God.
— Psalm 146:5

Happy are the people whose God is the Lord.
—Psalm 144:15

Blessed is the nation whose God is the Lord.
— Psalm 33:12

Forty times in the Old Testament alone, the Bible tells us that the state of the believer is one of happiness. Sometimes it is translated as happy, other times as blessed. Whatever the word, it means the same. Knowing the Lord, and knowing what He has done for us, should cause us to be the happiest people on Earth.

In his book, The Happiest People on Earth, Demos Shakarian says, "No matter what the condition of the world around us, we will be the happiest people on Earth."[2] However, as I said earlier, a lot of believers are not happy. What is the difference then between truly happy Christians and those who never experience the real joy of their salvation? I believe it is simpler than we may think.

In the book of Hosea we read,

My people are destroyed for lack of knowledge.
— Hosea 4:6

God gave us salvation through His Son Jesus Christ. Knowledge of all that salvation encompasses is found in His Word. However, if not studied and applied, this knowledge does nothing for us. It is the same in everything. If I had no knowledge of His saving grace, I could not have appropriated it for my life and I would still be lost and on my way to a place called Hell. But because knowledge was given to me by the preaching of His Word, I was able to make the decision to follow Jesus and be spared. If the only knowledge I have of my salvation is one of a life boat, or a ticket to Heaven, and I don't understand the impact of it on the present, then I will be like so many believers who try to fill the void of happiness with material things.

Please do not get the impression that material things are wrong. They are not. We read in the Word of God that He blesses us abundantly with material things if we allow Him to. God doesn't mind us having the things; He just doesn't want the things to have us.

Let me ask you something. Are you enjoying your life? I am not asking you if you have money or if all of your bills are paid. I am not even asking you if you have a lot of friends. But, I do want to know how you feel about your life right now. If you are like most people, you will say that for the most part you are enjoying life. But there are things you would like to change, right? The truth is, all of us would change something about our lives, and honestly, it will always be that way. There is always going to be something happening around you, or in your family, that is hard, negative, or hurtful. One of the surest ways to tell that you are still alive is the pain you feel. Christianity doesn't ignore life and all of its quirks and hurts, nor does it cover them up and act like they don't happen. Instead of ignoring life, it brings all that we long for to it; the peace we crave, the prosperity we desire, and the deliverance we need. Salvation is more than an event; it's more than a one time experience. It probably exceeds what you think it is right now. Salvation is a way of life. In fact, it is a new life altogether that began in a moment but lasts throughout eternity. It is the Father's perfect gift to us. It is His grace for every need - grace that can be called upon or drawn from.

Jesus created a great word picture when He related our born again experience to a well of life giving water.

> *"But the water that I shall give him shall be in him a well of water springing up into everlasting life."*
> *— John 4:14 KJV*

Knowledge of all salvation encompasses will help us to go deep into that well and draw out what we need. Isaiah spoke of this well when he said,

> *Therefore with joy you will draw water from the wells of salvation. — Isaiah 12:3*

Simply put, with an understanding of salvation comes the realization of what God has provided for us. It will allow us to create Heaven on Earth as we learn to draw out with joy what we need for every situation. No matter what curve life may throw at us, the home run will be hit by finding out what belongs to us and swinging away.

Consider this scripture found in the book of Psalms.

> *Blessed (happy, fortunate, to be envied) is he who has forgiveness of his transgression continually exercised upon him, whose sin is covered. Blessed (happy, fortunate, to be envied) is the man to whom the Lord imputes no iniquity and in whose spirit there is no deceit.* — Psalm 32:1-2 AMP

This verse of scripture could have just as easily read: Blessed, happy, fortunate, to be envied is the one who has been born again. That should be true of every Christian. I want every one of us to understand what happens when we receive Jesus Christ as Savior and how knowledge of this truth will help us to be the happiest people on Earth.

EXONERATE

ex-on-er-ate \ig-'zän-ə-,rāt\ to unburden, 1 : to relieve of a responsibility, obligation, or hardship 2 : to clear from accusation or blame

Chapter 2

———————●———————

Exonerative Realities

———————●———————

The very moment you or I made Jesus Christ the Lord of our lives, four very notable things happened. They are what I call the events of salvation. They are the one time events that took place when we were born again that caused the door to God to swing wide open for us. Although we may feel something emotionally, and usually do when this takes place, none of these events are based on emotions. I want to emphasize this because the emotions will wear off. Tomorrow will come, and you will have to deal with your flesh and other people as well. Knowing that all of the events of salvation happened because of what Jesus did, and not what we did or could do, will help us when facing the temptation to give up. When we wake up not feeling saved, or when the devil tries to tell us that we were never really saved at all, we can have peace in knowing that Jesus' blood forever settled our case before the Father. This peace directly corresponds to how much we know about our salvation, so let's get started in studying God's Word on the matter.

Four Events That Took Place When We Were Born Again

1. He redeemed us.

This simply means that Jesus bought us, or purchased us. Scripture clearly states in Acts 20:28 that the Church of God was purchased with His own blood - the blood of Jesus. We also see it in the book of Hebrews when we read the following:

> *Not with the blood of goats and calves, but with His own blood He entered the Most Holy Place once for all, having obtained eternal redemption.*
> *— Hebrews 9:12*

We do not use the word redeemed much anymore. Today it is more prevalent to say purchased, or bought, and this is exactly what Jesus did. He bought us. The Bible teaches us in the book of Ephesians that we were all under the dominion and lordship of Satan, and that we were all living in darkness. When Jesus shed His blood, He was at the same time paying the price of His blood to purchase our deliverance and freedom from Satan and his kingdom of darkness. Satan has no claim to you once you make Jesus Christ your Lord and Savior. In fact, the only tool he has against a born again Christian is deception. It is our responsibility to

> *Receive with meekness the implanted word, which is able to save your souls. — James 1:21*

Knowledge of the Word, and the application of the Word, is the only defense against the deception of the devil.

2. He remitted all that we have ever done.

Jesus has literally canceled everything that we have ever done that would cause us to deserve punishment. In other words, He declares us not guilty. Even the most sinful of sinners and the guiltiest of criminals are declared not guilty before God when they make Jesus Christ their Lord. The Bible says,

> *As far as the east is from the west, so far has He removed our transgressions from us.*
> *— Psalm 103:12*

Let's look at a few more scriptures that teach us along these lines. In the book of Romans, we read,

> *But now God has shown us a different way of being right in his sight - not by obeying the law but by the way promised in the Scriptures long ago. We are made right in God's sight when we trust in Jesus Christ to take away our sins. And we all can be saved in this same way, no matter who we are or what we have done. For all have sinned; all fall short of God's glorious standard. Yet now God in his gracious kindness declares us not guilty. He has done this through Christ Jesus, who has freed us by taking away our sins. — Romans 3:21-24 NLT*

I have never been arrested, nor have I had to go to court because of something I have done. So I can only imagine what it would be like to go before a judge while being guilty of a crime, only to have him declare me "not guilty!" This is what happened when we were saved. God the Father poured out the punishment for our crimes on His Son Jesus, and, in turn, declared us as not guilty and free from sin, placing us in a position of right-standing with Him.

3. He delivered us out of Satan's authority.

Really, it would have been enough if this were the end of His work, but He not only delivered us from Satan's authority, He also gave us authority over the work of the devil. This is where many Christians fail in their understanding about salvation. The Bible teaches us that when we were saved, the Holy Spirit came to live in us.

> *But you are not in the flesh but in the Spirit, if indeed the Spirit of God dwells in you. Now if anyone does not have the Spirit of Christ, he is not His. — Romans 8:9*

Someone far greater in power, strength, and authority has moved into us and set up permanent residence in our spirits. When He moved in, all that belongs to Him came with Him. This means that our authority as believers is backed by the same power that made the universe and the same authority that raised Jesus from the dead. It's no wonder that Satan is afraid of us finding out about this. He knows that when we do, his days are numbered as the governor of our lives. The Bible tells us in 1 John,

> *He who is in you is greater than he who is in the world. — 1 John 4:4*

I want you to really meditate on this verse. No matter how much Satan threatens you, or how much fear he sends your way, you can have the assurance that the Greater One is always with you. The Bible teaches us in Romans that if God is for us, who could be against us? I like to put it this way: If God is for me, what difference does it make who is against me?

Right after I committed my life to Jesus and answered the call to ministry, my wife and I experienced tough times in our relationship and in the financial realm as well. In just a matter of a few months, I had broken my arm, our house had caught on fire, both our vehicles were broken down, we were being sued for back taxes, and because of a very low paying job, we were way behind on all of our bills along with many obstacles I will not go into detail about. It was a miserable and very stressful time for both of us.

I specifically remember one day going to see a minister friend of mine. I was so stressed out that I did not know what to do next, so I went to see if he could help me by giving me some wisdom or advice. Remember, this was right after I had given my life to Jesus. I was a very young man, and a baby Christian. I considered my friend a very seasoned minister and mature in the faith. I will never forget what he told me that day.

"Douglas, what you need to do is get away and pray for a while and allow the Lord to show you if He is the One doing this to you, or if it is the devil. Sometimes," he said, "the Lord does these things to teach us something."

Even though I loved this man very much, and respected him for trying to help me, I can tell you right now that I left that place worse off than when I went in. I felt like my whole world was now turned upside down. I had come to Jesus because I needed help. I had cried out to Him for mercy, and now I had just found out that God may be the one causing all of my problems in the first place. I am ashamed to say this even today, but that set me back for a while because my thought life went in the direction that it was God doing all of this mean stuff to me. I became very depressed and frustrated because I felt like there was no one and no where I could turn to for help.

I am so thankful that in the midst of my ignorance and frustration, God Himself reached out to me. About two weeks later, another friend of mine introduced me to a business man from our community. David Terrell, still a friend to this day, began to mentor me in the things of God. I am most thankful for the eternal investment he made in my life. Although he owned a successful real estate company, he would always take time for me when I would go to see him.

I remember the first day I met David. He sat and listened to my story for a short while until he had heard enough that he made me pull out a Bible and read it - out loud! I had never done that before. He began to show me from the Word who I was, who Jesus was in me, and who I was in relationship with the Father. I still remember the first verse of scripture he made me read. It was Mark 11:22-23. It was then, and still remains, one of the most life changing revelations I have ever received. Not one time since that moment, when the Word went deep into my spirit man, have I ever doubted God's love and care for me. For one, it was the first time in my life I had read those particular verses of scripture. It was also the first time I had even imagined that God would give

authority to man. In the church that I attended, this
was never taught. Like so many believers today, I had
no idea about the things He had provided for me.
These verses in Mark literally opened up my spiritual
eyes to the truth that God has empowered man with
the same power and faith He gave to His Son Jesus. I
learned, for the first time, that it was Satan who was
afraid, for I was no longer under his dominion or lordship. Rather, I had been given authority over him by
Jesus Himself. Jesus said,

> *"Behold, I give you the authority to trample on
> serpents and scorpions, and over all the power of
> the enemy, and nothing shall by any means hurt
> you." — Luke 10:19*

This was some of the best news I had ever heard.

4. He recreated us.

This by far is the greatest, yet the most misunder-
stood, aspect of our salvation experience.

Let's first look at a few verses of scripture.

> *Therefore, if anyone is in Christ, he is a new
> creation; old things have passed away; behold,
> all things have become new. Now all things are
> of God, who has reconciled us to Himself
> through Jesus Christ, and has given us the min-
> istry of reconciliation, that is, that God was in
> Christ reconciling the world to Himself, not
> imputing their trespasses to them, and has
> committed to us the word of reconciliation.
> Now then, we are ambassadors for Christ, as
> though God were pleading through us: we*

*implore you on Christ's behalf, be reconciled to
God. For He made Him who knew no sin to be
sin for us, that we might become the righteousness of God in Him. — 2 Corinthians 5:17-21*

What a tremendous passage of scripture! If you are
a new believer reading this book right now, I want to
especially encourage you to meditate daily on these
scriptures. Having an understanding of this will cause
you to experience a much fuller and more fruitful life
than you ever thought possible. When you and I gain
understanding from the Word of God concerning how
we are to live, we begin to understand that we do not
have to be afraid anymore, nor do we have to battle
through life because of insecurities. This will cause us
to understand salvation as an event that gained our
entry into a new position in life.

A Good Position

If you are saved, you are a new creation. This really gives the idea that God takes a special interest in
each person individually. Actually, the word *new* in
verse 17 means just that. At the point of salvation, you
were uniquely made over. This word brings out two
meanings in the original Greek and indicates that we
were uniquely made both new in form and new in
substance. This would be like going to your favorite
car dealership to buy a new car that not only is new,
in that no one has ever driven it, but is new in the
sense that it is one of a kind as well. This is the
remarkable reason that a prostitute, who may have
been in that lifestyle for years, can be transformed into
a new creation and before God be as clean, pure, and

whole as a new born virgin daughter. It's this re-creation that places us in a unique position before the Father that is the same kind of position Jesus enjoyed while here on this earth, a position as one having never sinned. It's what I call a good position - a position that exceeds any we could possibly create for ourselves. Unlike a New Year's resolution that promises to do better or try harder, or a 12 step program that wears a past identity as a permanent label, being re-created in Christ Jesus affords us the awesome privilege of experiencing life with a clean slate and a new start. Glory to God! Old things have indeed been done away with, and we have been made new.

This verse of scripture also tells us that Jesus literally became sin for us so that we could become the righteousness of God in Christ Jesus. This means that He swapped positions with us. We were sinners who were separated from God, and He was in right standing with the Father. He took our place, and we took His. He became sin; we became righteous.

Let's look at a verse of scripture in the book of Isaiah.

> *I will greatly rejoice in the Lord, My soul shall be joyful in my God; For He has clothed me with the garments of salvation, He has covered me with the robe of righteousness.* — Isaiah 61:10

Jesus came to us. He reached out to us and gave us a gift we were unable to attain by our works. He gave us His righteousness to wear as a robe. The garment of works could not ever be sufficient in our quest to be one with the Father. That is the fault of all religions. Christianity is the only "religion" that reaches out to man and clothes him with the garments of salvation giving him the right to be a son of God. Consider the following scripture:

> *But you are a chosen generation, a royal priesthood, a holy nation, His own special people, that you may proclaim the praises of Him who called you out of darkness into His marvelous light.*
> *— 1 Peter 2:9*

In summary, let me review what Jesus did for us the moment we made Him Lord of our lives.

1. He redeemed us. (This means He bought us.)

2. He remitted all we have ever done. (This means we are no longer guilty of anything.)

3. He delivered us from Satan's authority. (This means that we do not ever have to be afraid of Satan for any reason at all.)

4. He recreated us. (This means He made us righteous. We are made right before the Father.)

EXPEL
ex-pel \ik-'spel\ 1 : to force out : EJECT
2 : to drive away; specif : DEPORT
3 : to cut off from membership

Chapter 3

•————————•

Expelling Limitations

•————————•

In chapter two, we saw what Jesus did for us at the event of salvation. Now, we want to look at what He is doing in us through the process of salvation. There is so much more to being saved than just getting your ticket to Heaven for the after-life. Jesus told us,

> *"I have come that they may have life, and that they may have it more abundantly."*
> *— John 10:10*

Jesus expects us to enjoy life right now while we are still here on this earth. Sure Heaven is going to be great and perfect. I am so thankful that I will be going there some day, but I also understand that what makes Heaven such a great place is that God is there. Well, I have great news for you. The same God that will be with us in Heaven is the same God who lives on the inside of us right now. Because of this, we can experience days of Heaven on Earth! I am not saying that it will always be perfect around us or even close to perfection. We are living on a planet that is experiencing many troubles through war, terrorism, and over-population. But because of the deposit the Spirit made inside us, guaranteeing our inheritance, we really can live a victorious life in the midst of trials, persecution, and even war. It is what happens in us, and our response to it, that makes us who we are, not what happens to us. Religion has taught man that there are limits to Christianity. It can only go so far when it comes to helping him. It tells him that all of the good things are reserved only for when he gets to Heaven. That is just not true.

As a pastor, I see the best and worst in people. There have been days when I would cry with one family and laugh with another. On the same day, while witnessing one person receiving the Lord, I would see another rejecting Him. Whether we are happy or sad, saved or unsaved, there are certain things we all crave that will only be found in Christ. I call them the seven desperations of humanity. They are the things that, if not addressed scripturally and correctly, will limit us to a mediocre life at best and prevent us from living our Christianity to the fullest. Let's look at each of these individually and see how Christ has become the answer for all of life's desperations.

The Seven Desperations

1. We desperately want to be happy.

Man's quest for happiness goes back to the Garden of Eden. God designed us to be happy. When death and the fear of death came into the earth because of Adam's sin and treason, man chose to find happiness from external circumstances. He chose to look to things and to other people in order to be happy. But now, because of what Jesus did for us in restoring us to a relationship with the Father, happiness is found within. Now, I can be happy regardless of the things I have or the people I am surrounded by. Happiness comes because I know Him, and best of all, He knows me.

2. We desperately want to be free from the hurt.

As I stated previously, someone once said that the only sure sign that we are alive is the pain we feel. We have all tried many different things to cover it up instead of really dealing with it the right way. Sin has caused much pain in the earth. All of the things we have done wrong and the things that have been done to us cause us to experience this pain. The abuse many grew up with, the molestation, the anger, the emotional scars that run deep, have scarred our hearts. And for more people than ever before, the only coping mechanism is medication. I am not condemning its use; however, medication often only numbs the pain instead of healing its source. In contrast, there are some people who don't want to numb the pain; rather, they want to inflict further pain on themselves or others. This becomes evident when people use anger, revenge, or other self-destructive behaviors to try to deal with the pain, but it only makes things worse.

This reminds me of what happened to John Kennedy, Jr. He was killed in a plane crash a few years ago, as most will remember because of the headlines it made. According to the FAA and the radar tracking, the aircraft was in a "graveyard spiral" which is a virtual free fall at 4000 feet per minute. Usually, this will cause the pilot to lose horizon and become disoriented. The g-forces cause you to be unable to determine whether you are upside down, sideways, or upright. When you realize what is happening, the natural tendency is to do exactly the opposite of what you need to do. You are diving so rapidly that you think you should throttle up, accelerate, and pull up, but this will only cause you to spiral faster. The real solution is to let off of the accelerator and straighten out the wings. Doing what may seem natural can get you killed as in the case of John Kennedy, Jr.

The Bible says,

> *There is a way which seems right to a man, and appears straight before him, but the end of that way is death.* — *Proverbs 14:12 AMP*

It may seem natural to isolate ourselves, abuse our own bodies, or lash out at others to try to cope with the pain of life, but gratification resulting from these actions will only be short-lived, and ultimately, destruction will come. True recovery from every hurt and pain is found only in the healing mercies of Jesus Christ.

3. We desperately want to be free from guilt.

Guilt is the result of two things: not forgiving others and not being forgiven. Guilt is dangerous because it can make the nicest of people turn vicious. When you received Jesus as your Savior, He cleansed you from anything and everything you had done in the past. You have to accept this forgiveness and stop allowing those feelings of guilt to control you any longer. It does not matter what you have done. Oh, you may have to face consequences for certain things, such as breaking the law, but when it comes to being born again and free from guilt, Jesus made it possible.

I am reminded of a story I heard a preacher tell once about Stephen Morin. Stephen Morin was executed in Texas on March 13, 1985 for murder. At one time he was on the FBI's Most Wanted list. Although he committed some horrible crimes and justice was served in his death, I believe he is in Heaven today. The story goes that he had abducted a lady named Margaret Palm from a store one day with the intention of killing her. One thing Stephen had not counted on was that Mrs. Palm was a Spirit-filled believer. After several hours, she led Stephen to the Lord, and he eventually turned himself in to the authorities. In prison, he led many others to the Lord before he was executed. It was said that he looked forward to his death calling it a "graduation". His last words were, "Heavenly Father, I give thanks for this time, for the time that we have been together, the fellowship in Your Word, and the Christian family presented to me [naming the witnesses]. Allow Your Holy Spirit to flow as I know your love has been showered upon me. Forgive them for they know not what they do, as I know that you have forgiven me, as I have forgiven them. Lord Jesus, I commit my soul to you. I praise you, and I thank you."[1]

This story has always been a reminder to me of the simple truth that no matter what I have done, or how bad I have been, I was forgiven by the God of Heaven, and I am now not guilty!

4. We desperately want to be free from emptiness and a lack of self-worth.

People want to feel valued. We all want to be able to add something by being here. One of the reasons Rick Warren's book, *The Purpose Driven Life*,[2] sold so many copies is because people are looking for a purpose. His book helps them to answer the question, Why am I here?

Life with Jesus will bring true fulfillment and worth. It's in Him that we are made complete. Only Jesus can fill the void and emptiness that we have had since birth. And only His Spirit can lead us into a life filled with purpose.

5. We desperately want to be free from loneliness.

It was never God's intention for man to go through life alone. From the beginning of creation, man was placed with other people. Marriages, family villages, and cities are all in the plan of God for everyone. Because of sin and the separation it brings, people can still feel lonely although surrounded by others. Sometimes the loneliest of times are when we are part of a crowd. Knowledge that God is a person who wants to have a close relationship with each one of us is an enormous comfort. After all, He is

> *...a friend who sticks closer than a brother.*
> *— Proverbs 18:24*

6. We desperately want to not be afraid anymore.

Fear is by far the single most motivating factor for

all of humanity's actions and responses. Fear is meant to paralyze. It is meant to stop us. Satan uses fear to stop us from trusting God. If we allow him to, he will use fear in order to prevent us from fulfilling the very plan God has for us.

Fear causes us to do all kinds of negative and self-destructive things. All co-dependency, insecurity, anxiety, lack of trust, and many diseases are rooted in fear - all of which Jesus wants to deliver us from. 1 John 4:18 says, "Perfect love casts out fear." As we grow in the knowledge of His love for us, we will experience freedom from fear.

7. *We desperately want to go to Heaven when we die.*

Regardless of what anyone says in their arrogance, or ignorance for that matter, everyone wants to go to Heaven when they die. No one in their right mind would want to ever go to a place like the Bible describes as Hell. Jesus told us in John,

> *"Let not your heart be troubled; you believe in God, believe also in Me. In My Father's house are many mansions; if it were not so, I would have told you. I go to prepare a place for you. And if I go and prepare a place for you, I will come again and receive you to Myself; that where I am, there you may be also. And where I go you know, and the way you know." Thomas said to Him, "Lord, we do not know where You are going, and how can we know the way?" Jesus said to him, "I am the way, the truth, and the life. No one comes to the Father except through Me." — John 14:1-6*

Jesus has been preparing a place for us for over 2000 years. Only through Him can we have the assurance of a home in Heaven.

In conclusion, there is only one thing that will really make us happy, remove the pain, free the guilt, fill the emptiness, remove the fear, destroy the loneliness, and ensure our place in Heaven. It is when we accept the sacrifice that God made in His Son, Jesus Christ, and make Him our Lord.

EXCHANGE

ex-change \iks-'chānj\ *1: the act of giving or taking one thing in return for another : TRADE 2: the act of substituting one thing for another*

Chapter 4

---•---

Exchanging The Old

---•---

Earlier, we learned that we were a new creation the very moment Jesus came into our hearts. What we are going to do in this chapter is elaborate further along these lines. Remember that when we were saved, Jesus purchased a position for us before the Father. It is a good position - a position much like He enjoyed while He was on this earth. It's called righteousness. Righteousness, or being right, does not mean that you do everything right. It's not about what you do or don't do, but it is a position of rightness given by God because of His favor toward us.

I want to give you a definition of what it means to be righteous. *Righteousness is the ability to stand in the presence of the Father without a sense of guilt, condemnation, or inferiority.*[1] It is the good position we have before the Heavenly Father that allows us to speak to Him as a child would speak to his or her father. It produces the confidence to stand in the presence of men, and even Satan, without fear or insecurity.

Jesus stood in this position and purchased our right to be in right-standing before the Father. Let's look further into how Jesus stood before the Father, before the devil, and before the storm.

Before the Father

Concerning Lazarus, John wrote,

Then they took away the stone from the place where the dead man was lying. And Jesus lifted up His eyes and said, "Father, I thank You that You have heard Me. And I know that You always hear Me, but because of the people who are standing by I said this, that they may believe that You sent Me." Now when He had said these things, He cried with a loud voice, "Lazarus, come forth!" And he who had died came out bound hand and foot with graveclothes, and his face was wrapped with a cloth. Jesus said to them, "Loose him, and let him go." — John 11:41-44

Before the devil

And the devil said to Him, "If You are the Son of God, command this stone to become bread." But Jesus answered him, saying, "It is written, 'Man shall not live by bread alone, but by every word of God.'" Then the devil, taking Him up on a high mountain, showed Him all the kingdoms of the world in a moment of time. And the devil said to Him, "All this authority I will give You, and their glory; for this has been delivered to me, and I give it to whomever I wish. Therefore, if You will worship before me, all will be Yours." And Jesus answered and said to him, "Get behind Me, Satan! For it is written, 'You shall worship the Lord your God, and Him only you shall serve'." — Luke 4:3-8

Exchanging The Old

Before the storm

*Then He arose and rebuked the wind, and said to
the sea, "Peace, be still!" And the wind ceased and
there was a great calm. But He said to them, "Why
are you so fearful? How is it that you have no
faith?" And they feared exceedingly, and said to
one another, "Who can this be, that even the wind
and the sea obey Him!" — Mark 4:39-41*

Jesus' understanding of His position before the
Father caused Him to be a master over circumstances.
Our understanding of the position He wrought for us
will help us stand before any and all obstacles with
the confidence that knows the same One Who helped
Jesus is the One Who is helping us.

In his book, *Two Kinds of Righteousness*, E.W.
Kenyon states the following:

*"We have become the righteousness of God in
Him, but we have been living as slaves when we
ought to reign as kings. We yielded without a
fight when we heard the adversary roar about
our unworthiness to stand in God's presence."[2]*

What a powerfully profound statement.
Understanding our position of righteousness is one of
the greatest needs of the Church today. In fact, knowing who we are in Christ, how the Father looks at us,
and what He considers us to be, should be the fun-
damental truths a person is taught upon entering into
the Kingdom of God. The unfortunate thing is that
because so much of our teaching nowadays is based

on feelings and emotions, most believers are never taught who they are in Christ, nor do they have an understanding of being made righteous. Instead, they continue to live life after being born again with their thoughts and understanding governed by the old sin nature. Believers still think, act, and speak just like they did before they were born again. We know this because of the problems people are still having and the issues they struggle with long after they have been saved.

Before we look thoroughly at what it means to have a consciousness and perception of being righteous, let's look at a few indicators that tell us if we are still living according to a sin nature, or with a sin consciousness. I am going to ask several questions, and if the answer to any of them is yes, you would benefit immensely from renewing your mind to righteousness.

1. Do you feel unworthy to approach the Heavenly Father?

I am not asking whether you pray or not. I am asking if you feel you are unworthy of His love and care. In the book of 2 Corinthians, the Bible states,

"Therefore, come out from among them and be separate," says the Lord. "Do not touch what is unclean, and I will receive you. I will be a Father to you, and you shall be My sons and daughters," says the Lord Almighty. — 2 Corinthians 6:17-18

We are not (as some teach) unclean, undeserving, unworthy, worms, or filthy rags. We were these things, but now we are the sons and daughters of the Most High God, and it is time we approach Him based on who we really are, and not how we feel. In verse 14 of the same chapter, we are told,

> *Do not be unequally yoked together with unbe-*
> *lievers. For what fellowship has righteousness*
> *with lawlessness? And what communion has*
> *light with darkness? — 2 Corinthians 6:14*

Do you see what this verse is saying? Here we are called righteous, and we are called light. He is saying that perfect communion can only take place when it is between two like persons. He is light, and we are light. He is righteous; likewise we are righteous. He is worthy, and because of what Jesus did, we have been made worthy. Do not ever be ashamed to approach the Father. As a matter of fact, even when you have messed up or sinned, learn to run to Him instead of running from Him. This is where most people misunderstand how much our Father loves us. His love is everlasting, longsuffering, and unconditional. Most of us believe this is true, yet our actions - especially when we run from Him - say that we believe His love comes with conditions. It is in those times of failure, though, when we feel least deserving of His kindness and favor toward us, that we more fully appreciate and comprehend the depth of His unfailing and unwavering love.

2. *When you pray, is asking forgiveness the first thing you do?*

Christians with more of an understanding of their sin, and not His favor and love, usually begin every prayer by asking the Lord to forgive them. In this context, I am not dealing with repentance. Repentance and forgiveness are vital to our spiritual health and well-being (see 1 John 1:9). But remember, what I'm dealing with here is a sin consciousness. Does your awareness of your sins, faults, and failures dominate your praying? Do you have confidence to use your authority to be on the offense in prayer against the works of darkness? Can you boldly pray the Word of God over yourself and others, or are you consumed with shortcomings?

Do you have sin in your life? Certainly, we all do, but does the constant awareness of that sin hinder you from a confident, power-filled prayer-life? If so, go to the Word of God in Romans 8:1 which states that there is now no condemnation to those who are in Christ Jesus. The Spirit of God is not accusing you or condemning you. That is the work of the devil. If you have repented of your sin - that means you have turned from it - then you are free from it. God has forgiven you and forgotten your sin. It is vital to your relationship with Him that you do the same.

3. Do you find it more comfortable to have someone else pray for you?

Thousands of believers flock to meetings and crusades every year to have someone pray for them. Others flock to altars to have their pastors and church leaders pray for them. This in itself is not a problem. Ministry received through well-known evangelists, prophets, and prominent church leaders is valuable and vital. God gave these ministry gifts to us for our good. But, it is wrong to think that God will hear them and not hear us. The blood of Jesus ensured an open door to the Father to all who believe - not just high profile Christian personalities with television ministries or large followings. Jeremiah 33:3 says, "**[You]** call unto me and I will answer **you** and show **you** great and mighty things which **you** do not know" (emphasis mine).

4. Do you believe you are a sinner saved by grace?

One of the biggest fallacies the Church has swallowed hook, line, and sinker over the last 100 years is that we are all nothing more than sinners saved by grace. Not one time in the New Covenant is a Christian called a sinner. To the contrary, Christians are addressed as saints, as the Righteous, as a Glorious Church, and as the Church of the Living God. We *were* sinners who were saved by grace, but we are no longer sinners after we receive the grace, acceptance, and love of God. We are, in fact, the favored of the Lord. We will discuss the grace we have in Christ in a later chapter.

5. Are you insecure in your walk with God?

Wondering if your prayers are heard is common among many Christians, but that is not how God intends for us to live. It will hinder effective praying. In order to overcome this insecurity, we must renew our minds to the Word of God. Let's look at a verse of scripture in the book of 1 John.

Now this is the confidence that we have in Him, that if we ask anything according to His will, He hears us. And if we know that He hears us, what-

ever we ask, we know that we have the petitions that we have asked of Him. — 1 John 5:14-15

We can have confidence because we know that He hears us. We know because He told us in His Word. We must believe His Word and act accordingly.

6. Do you feel guilty when you have not prayed enough, given enough, or suffered enough?

Many believers are still trying to pay for their sin through penance, just as monks tried to do during the monastic age. Sometimes believers still feel they owe God. This turns grace into something other than a free gift. Colossians 2:14 tells us that the debt that was against us has been canceled or blotted out. Works could not pay it - only the blood of Jesus was sufficient. Simply stated, I owed a debt for my sin. Jesus paid it in full, and it can never be held against me again. Hallelujah!

7. Do you feel like God would never use you?

Another way of asking this question would be, do you feel like God could ever use you? Sometimes we are so conscious of our faults that we think we are unusable. We have thoughts about it being too late for us or that we're too old or that we've done too much or gone too far and can never go back. But, thank God, we have His Word to go back to. It tells us of the prodigal son who, after a season of sin and misery, came to his senses and returned home to his father's house (Luke 15:11-32). The Word also tells us of Peter denying Jesus and of Jesus' love for Peter. Jesus forgave him and instructed him to feed

His sheep. After utter failure, Peter was restored in his relationship with the Father and was entrusted with a world changing ministry (see John 13, 18, 21 and Acts 2).

8. Do you reach for your Bible last when faced with the difficulties of life?

In a country where seemingly everything is at our fingertips, it is easy to rely on God last or not at all. Think about it. We have every kind of medication, doctor, therapist, counselor, book, pamphlet, church, religion, internet site, and opinion known to man, so it is easy to get into the mode of putting God last. But God wants to be our first resort and for His Word to be the final authority in our lives. Don't wait until the storm comes to find out who He is or what His will is. Turn to Him now. In Matthew, Jesus says,

> *"But seek first the kingdom of God and His right-eousness, and all these things shall be added to you."* — *Matthew 6:33*

Quit seeking after everything else and learn to seek Him above all else. He will take care of the rest.

9. Do you believe God heals today but doubt He will heal you?

This is huge with so many Christians. Most would agree that God does heal today; they are just unsure that He would heal them. We have to know the Bible and what it says about healing for ourselves. The reason I bring this up is because healing was such a vital part of the ministry of Jesus and is provided for in the atonement. Let's look at a verse of scripture found in Matthew.

> *That it might be fulfilled which was spoken by Isaiah the prophet, saying: "He Himself took our infirmities and bore our sicknesses."*
> — *Matthew 8:17*

The same God who forgives all your iniquities also heals all your diseases (see Psalm 103:3).

10. Are you afraid to say certain things because the devil might hear you?

I mention this because it hinders so many Christians from standing in their place of authority. In our own strength, we can do nothing, but clothed in righteousness, and covered by the blood of Jesus, we are more than conquerors (Romans 8:37). I want you to say something right now out loud. Say this, "I have authority over the devil! He is a defeated foe and can do nothing to me." Don't worry. He really has been paralyzed by what Jesus did. As far as the devil's power and authority are concerned, he is a little bitty devil, and you and I have a great big God living on the inside of us!

If you answered yes...

The truth is, most of us would answer yes to at least one of these questions. If you did, it does not mean you are a bad person. It just means that you, and for that matter we, need to renew our minds to the truth of God's Word concerning who we are and how He views us. So, let's take a look at several scriptures that teach us about this position. I want to warn you, though. Once you find out the truth concerning this good position you are in, you'll probably never be the same again. It changed me, and my prayer is that you will experience the same life change as well.

We were made righteous.

Let's begin with a verse of scripture found in 2 Corinthians.

> *For He made Him who knew no sin to be sin for us, that we might become the righteousness of God in Him. — 2 Corinthians 5:21*

This verse tells us that Jesus literally became sin for us, so that we could become what He is: the righteousness of God. Remember, Jesus swapped places with us. He took the beatings, the crucifixion, the death, and the separation from the Father that we deserved and put us in a good position before the Father, one like only He experienced. He literally exchanged positions with us.

Why has He done this for us? I believe one reason is because God wants us to rule and reign with Him. This may be a new concept for some, but look at the following scripture also in 2 Corinthians.

> *Now then, we are ambassadors for Christ, as though God were pleading through us: we implore you on Christ's behalf, be reconciled to God. — 2 Corinthians 5:20*

Notice the word *ambassador*. An ambassador is someone with high rank that stands in the place of another high ranking individual, representing one government to another.[3] The Apostle Paul is saying that he is on official business representing the government of the Kingdom of Heaven, standing in the place of Jesus Himself. And this is what we are supposed to be doing. You see, with this understanding that as we go, we are backed by the High Court of Heaven, we are able to be much more confident as we do the business of our Father.

Ruling and Reigning

God has always desired that man rule, reign, and represent Him in the world. This is brought out even more when we look in the book of 2 Timothy.

> *If we endure, we shall also reign with Him.*
> *— 2 Timothy 2:12*

This verse brings out our role in an amazing way. The word *reign* in this verse means to be a co-regent. The definition of a co-regent is "one who governs a kingdom in the absence of a sovereign".[4] If this verse was referring to later - when we get to Heaven - then another word would have been used. When we get to Heaven, God will not be absent in the way He is now. Now, we know Him in part, and the down payment of His Spirit has been given to us. But then, we will know and see Him face to face. So until that time, let's take the role and position of righteousness that He gave to us, and with confidence and authority, go forth boldly declaring the works of our God!

The Bottom Line

Exchanging the old is not just a clever way to say "old things are passed away" in the sense that old sins are gone or that carnal, fleshly living is over. It means the old creature wasn't sufficient to function in the grace of God, so God made a new creature that was. Before our Father, we are brand new. We must allow the Word of God to transform our thinking and therefore, transform our living. We must live as ambassadors, joint heirs, and co-regents. We are the righteousness of God in Christ.

EXTRAVAGANT
ex-trav-a-gant \ik-'strav-i-gˀnt\ *1: a : WANDERING b : STRANGE CURIOUS 2 a : exceeding the limits of reason or necessity b : extremely or excessively elaborate c : PROFUSE*

Chapter 5

---•---

Extravagant Creation

---•---

Psalm 8 is a great chapter that begins to describe prophetically God's view of man. We get the impression that David wrote it while still a young shepherd boy out tending his father's sheep. This psalm, like many that were written by him, begins with praise and exaltation to the Lord. A question is asked by David, and then the Lord answers prophetically through David himself. Let's look at the whole psalm.

> *O Lord, our Lord, How excellent is Your name in all the earth, Who have set Your glory above the heavens! Out of the mouth of babes and nursing infants You have ordained strength, because of Your enemies, that You may silence the enemy and the avenger. When I consider Your heavens, the work of Your fingers, the moon and the stars, which You have ordained, what is man that You are mindful of him, and the son of man that You visit him? For You have made him a little lower than the angels, and You have crowned him with glory and honor. You have made him to have dominion over the works of Your hands; You*

*have put all things under his feet, all sheep and
oxen - even the beasts of the field, the birds of the
air, and the fish of the sea that pass through the
paths of the seas. O Lord, our Lord, how excellent
is Your name in all the earth! — Psalm 8:1-9*

The question, "What is man that you are mindful
of him?" is one that most people have asked in one
form or another. To translate it in a more contempo-
rary way, we might ask, "God, in all that there is and
all you have created throughout the universe, why do
you give your best attention to man?" I remember
where I was when I first began to understand what
David was feeling when he wrote this psalm. A few
years ago my wife, Debbie, and I went on a mission
trip to Peru. Our trip took us up the Amazon River to
one of its tributaries deep in the Amazonian forest.
Late one evening, Debbie and I decided to go up to
the deck of the boat that was taking us into the jun-
gle. The sky was amazing! Since there was very little
pollution, it was clearer than I had ever seen. A beau-
tiful black blanket laden with bright yellow and white
stars and the outline of the Milky Way was a stunning
sight to see. It is something that I will never forget. It
was at that time I remember telling Debbie that with
all of creation that we see, and even much more that
we can't, God has still chosen to give His greatest
attention to man. It's almost unbelievable. But, just
like Paul's prayer in Ephesians tells us, the destination
point for God's power is us. Let's look at that verse.

*And what is the exceeding greatness of His
power toward us who believe, according to the
working of His mighty power. — Ephesians 1:19*

He is telling us that the exceeding, unusual magnitude of God's ability and might has a destination, and that destination is you and me. Praise the Lord!

Now, let's look again at Psalm chapter 8. There are four things that the psalmist brings out that I want us to examine here.

He made us a little lower than angels?

First, he says in verse four that we were made a little lower than angels. The word used for angels in this verse is also used 218 times in the book of Genesis. The only problem with this is that in Genesis, it was translated to English as God. It is the Hebrew word Elohiym. It is pronounced *el-o-heem*. It is God in plural form. In Genesis we read,

> *In the beginning, **God** created the heavens and the earth. — Genesis 1:1 (emphasis mine)*

A more literal translation would read, ***In the beginning God the Father, God the Son, and God the Holy Spirit created the heavens and the earth.***

So, in reality, the Word teaches us that we were made a little lower than God. It couldn't possibly be angels since Paul tells us later that angels will be judged by us.

> *Do you not know that we shall judge angels? — 1 Corinthians 6:3*

So contrary to what you have heard or what religion has taught you, God created you to be a little lower than Himself. You are not God, nor are you deity, but you do have a place of authority - authority to build the kingdom of God and authority over the

works of the devil. This has been discussed in previous chapters, but it bears much repetition.

He crowned us with glory and honor.

Secondly, he tells us that God crowns us with
glory and honor. Maybe you do not feel like you are
honored, but think about this for a moment: The
human is the only being created that can choose to
improve not only himself but his surroundings and
other humans as well. All other life forms on Earth
either depend on humans for their quality of life or
cannot improve their quality of life outside of natural
instincts. We have received honor from the Lord that
allows us to choose to improve anything we want to
improve. We can live anywhere, in any culture, with
any terrain. We are creative, ingenious, imaginative,
and pioneering. We possess these attributes because
the Lord chose to honor us with the ultimate honor -
freedom of choice. He favors and trusts humanity to
such a degree that He allows us to make our own
choices concerning His planet and His creation. He
said to be fruitful and multiply, and then he uniquely gifted each individual to fulfill his or her purpose.
He honored us with diversity, and He delights in it.

He also crowns us with glory. Think of it. We
have been made to literally house the glory of God.
Isaiah says,

> *Arise, shine; for your light has come! And the*
> *glory of the Lord is risen upon you. — Isaiah 60:1*

We were created to live in and be filled with the
glory of God. When Adam fell, we were separated

from it. But Jesus restored us and brought many sons to glory (see Hebrews 2:10).

He gave us dominion.

Thirdly, he tells us in verse five that God gave us dominion over all of the works of His hands. In order to really get the full measure of this, we will have to go back to the original creation in Genesis. We need to see how God set this thing up from the very beginning in order to understand what His will is for mankind. In the book of Genesis, we read:

> *Then God said, "Let Us make man in Our image, according to Our likeness; let them have dominion over the fish of the sea, over the birds of the air, and over the cattle, over all the earth and over every creeping thing that creeps on the earth." So God created man in His own image; in the image of God He created him; male and female He created them. Then God blessed them, and God said to them, "Be fruitful and multiply; fill the earth and subdue it; have dominion over the fish of the sea, over the birds of the air, and over every living thing that moves on the earth."*
> *— Genesis 1:26-28*

According to this passage, God began by making man like Him and in His image. It is His intention that we act and look like God. As you have heard, we are the only Jesus some will ever see. We are His representation on this earth. But I want to pay special attention to what He said about our role on this planet. He said, "Let them have dominion." In other words, we were created to have dominion over everything else He created.

He put all things under our feet.

Lastly, we are told that He has put all things under our feet. This point is brought out when we read what Paul said about it in Ephesians.

And He put all things under His feet, and gave Him to be head over all things to the church, which is His body. — Ephesians 1:22-23

Furthermore, Paul says in chapter two,

And raised us up together, and made us sit together in the heavenly places in Christ Jesus. — Ephesians 2:6

In these verses of scripture, we see that Jesus was given authority and dominion, and we also see that He gave us authority and dominion.

What a tremendous responsibility and opportunity we have. One of these days we will be judged by what we have done with the position of honor and dominion He gave us. Are we using our position to better our planet? Have we used it to reach more people for Christ? With all of the tools that have been given to us with this position - the Word, the blood and name of Jesus, the Church, the Holy Spirit, and His gifts - what kind of stewards will we be judged as? I, for one, want to be found faithful and obedient to my calling as a believer. Did I walk worthy as one who stands in a good position of authority, or did I walk powerless and defeated? God the Father has provided every resource I need to walk in victory. I must choose to take a stand of faith because it is ultimately my choice.

EXHIBIT
ex-hib-it \iq-'zib- t\ *1 : to present to view : as a : to show or display outwardly esp. by visible signs or actions b : to show publicly esp. for purposes of competition or demonstration*

Chapter 6

———————•———————

Exhibitive Realities

———————•———————

The opportunity to be born again is the greatest gift ever given to humanity. There is so much to being saved and so much we won't even realize until we get to Heaven. The Bible tells us in the book of Ephesians:

> *That in the ages to come He might show the exceeding riches of His grace in His kindness toward us in Christ Jesus. — Ephesians 2:7*

Even with all we know about the grace of God and His favor toward us, it will literally take ages and ages for the Father to show us all He has done for us in and through Christ Jesus and how much He loves us. But that is all in the plan He has for us. From the very beginning of man, God has been showing Himself - all He is and has - to us.

When the Father revealed Himself, He chose to dwell among us, as one of us. He, the Word, took on flesh, coming in the form of the Son of God. He was called Jesus Christ, or Jesus, the Anointed One, sent from God, the Father. As the Son of God, he had a job description. In John, Jesus said,

"My food is to do the will of Him who sent me and to finish His work." — John 4:34

Jesus finished His work as the sacrifice for sin. He defeated death, hell, and the grave when He rose from the dead. But when He ascended into Heaven, His work wasn't complete. He is still working on our behalf as the head of the Church (see Ephesians 1:20-23). He is the head, or CEO, if you will, and as such, He is still working in the following areas:

- Building His Church by pouring out the Holy Spirit to all those who believe (Acts 2:32-33, 38-39).

- Interceding for us as our mediator (Hebrews 7:24, 25; Romans 8:34).

- Giving grace to all believers (Ephesians 4:7).

- Giving strength and protection to His people (2 Thessalonians 3:3; Philippians 4:13).

- Giving revelation, insight, and understanding to His people (Galatians 1:11,12).

- Giving ministries to the Body and the world (Ephesians 4:11-13).

- Eagerly anticipating meeting all of us in the air and taking us to our heavenly home (Philippians 3:20,21; 1 Thessalonians 4:15-18).

I could take any one of these points and elaborate on them extensively. Each, on its own, is worthy of much in-depth discussion, but for the rest of this chapter, I want to focus on one thing: What is God, through His Holy Spirit, doing in us right now? In other words, how is Jesus building His Church through the present day ministry of the Holy Spirit?

First of all, let me establish that Jesus was dependent upon the power of the Holy Spirit in His own ministry. In Luke, Jesus said,

> *"The Spirit of the Lord is upon Me, because He has anointed Me to preach the gospel to the poor; He has sent Me to heal the brokenhearted, to proclaim liberty to the captives and recovery of sight to the blind, to set at liberty those who are oppressed; to proclaim the acceptable year of the Lord." — Luke 4:18-19*

Speaking of Jesus, John said,

> *"I saw the Spirit descending from heaven like a dove, and he [the Spirit] remained upon Him [Jesus]." — John 1:32 (emphasis mine)*

Before the water baptism of Jesus, John had been instructed by God the Father concerning the identity of the Son of God. He said,

> *"Upon whom you see the Spirit descending, and remaining on Him, This is He who baptizes with the Holy Spirit." — John 1:33*

In these passages, it is evident that the Spirit of the Lord was upon Jesus and that Jesus was the One who would baptize believers with the Holy Spirit. Other terminology is used in scripture to describe Jesus' interaction with the Holy Spirit. For example, in John 20:22, Jesus breathed on His disciples and told them to receive the Holy Spirit. In Luke, He said to His disciples,

> *"Behold, I send the promise of My Father upon you; but tarry in the city of Jerusalem until you are endued with power from on high." — Luke 24:49*

In John 16:7, speaking of the Holy Spirit, Jesus says,

> *"Nevertheless, I tell you the truth. It is to your advantage that I go away; for if I do not go away, the Helper will not come to you; but if I depart, I will send Him to you." — John 16:7*

In these verses of scripture, we see that Jesus *baptizes* with the Spirit, instructs disciples to *receive* the Spirit, and promises to *send* the Spirit. In Luke, we see that this was the plan, or promise, of the Father. In sending the Spirit, or baptizing believers with the Spirit, Jesus was and is carrying out the work of the Father who sent Him.

In John 16, Jesus referred to the Holy Spirit as our Helper. Since Jesus could not remain on the earth, He sent His Spirit in His place to help us. We will now look at how He helps us in our daily walk, once we've been born again, by giving us access to the Father's grace and by revealing the Father's glory in us and through us.

The Holy Spirit Gives Access to the Father's Grace

Total access to our Heavenly Father is given to us by the Holy Spirit who lives in us. This privilege was given to us under the New Covenant. In the book of Ephesians, the Bible teaches:

> *For through Him we both have access by one Spirit to the Father. Now, therefore, you are no longer strangers and foreigners, but fellow citizens with the saints and members of the household of God.*
> — *Ephesians 2:18-19*

God never will ask us who we are when we approach Him because we are His children. Jesus purchased with His blood our right to go to our Father any time and for any occasion. The way has been paved. In Hebrews, the Bible spells it out with even more clarity when it says,

> *Let us therefore come boldly to the throne of grace that we may obtain mercy and find grace to help in time of need.* — *Hebrews 4:16*

I know some of you may be thinking about how wonderful that is. We have access to the One Who created the Universe. He cares for us individually. He asks us to come to Him with boldness. The word *boldly* found in this scripture carries with it an attitude. It means to approach Him with frankness and with the assurance that He hears us. Our relationship with the Heavenly Father operates in the same way that a healthy father-child relationship would. All that

I have and own is His, and all that He has and is belongs to me; therefore, I can have confidence in His presence.

But, what does it mean to obtain grace? Many times when we hear grace preached or taught, the phrase **unmerited favor** is used, and rightfully so. God gives grace to us not because of our works, but because of the finished work of Jesus. We did not deserve it, but He graces us anyway. Many times when grace is taught, the whole emphasis is on the unmerited part, and not on the grace part. Here, I am going to focus on the grace part. After all, it is the grace of God that is at work in you right now. So what does it mean to have access to His grace? First, let's look at what grace is. Grace means favor. To say God gives us grace is to say He favors us. But I want us to look at this a little more in detail as well.

To say that God favors us is to say that He willingly uses His ability for us. We all know God is able. Many sermons preached nowadays are about the ability of God. But it does us no good at all to just know He is able. We must know He is willing to use that ability on our behalf. More scripture tells us about His willingness than about His ability. That's what grace is; it's God willingly using His strength, power, and ability to help in time of need.

Religion may tell us that God is able or that God can. It may preface all prayers with the statement, "If it be Thy will". It may proclaim from pulpits across America, "You never know what God is going to do!" But grace shouts, "God is able! And He is willing to use that ability for you!" Grace boldly declares, "I know His will because I know His Word." It will always cry out that God has provided all that He is and all that He has for those who follow Him.

Thank God, we have access to this grace of our loving Father through the blood of His Son. What a good position we stand in! What an awesome privilege we have as children of God! But don't think for a minute that our access to His grace is only for our benefit. Not hardly. It is to glorify God. This brings us to the next point.

The Holy Spirit Reveals and Reflects the Glory of God

Let's look at 2 Corinthians 3:18 in several translations.

> *But we all, with unveiled face, beholding as in a mirror the glory of the Lord, are being transformed into the same image from glory to glory, just as by the Spirit of the Lord.*
> *— 2 Corinthians 3:18*

> *And all of us, as with unveiled face, [because we] continued to behold [in the Word of God] as in a mirror the glory of the Lord, are constantly being transfigured into His very own image in ever increasing splendor and from one degree of glory to another; [for this comes] from the Lord [Who is] the Spirit.*
> *— 2 Corinthians 3:18 AMP*

I especially like how this verse reads in the New Living Translation.

And all of us have had that veil removed so that we can be mirrors that brightly reflect the glory of the Lord. And as the Spirit of the Lord works within us, we become more and more like Him and reflect His glory even more.
— 2 Corinthians 3:18 NLT

The first reference this scripture gives is one that relates back to Moses. In Exodus 34, we are taught that Moses had to place a veil over his face because of the glory of God causing his face to shine. He had invested so much time with the Lord that it affected his flesh. This shining caused the children of Israel to fear him so that when he was speaking to the Israelites, he would cover his face, but when speaking to God, he would remove the veil. The Bible tells us in this verse that we will change too, but not like Moses did. Instead of the glory changing our face and skin, we are changed from the inside-out, transformed into an image that looks like Him. This is what the Spirit is doing right now in us if we will allow Him to. As we walk with Him and commune with Him, meditating on His Word, the Bible teaches that two things will happen.

1. God's glory is reflected to Him.

We will reflect back to God His own glory and majesty as we allow Him to work in us a metamorphosis, or transformation, from what we used to be to what we are supposed to be - like Him. A great verse of scripture that really brings this out is found in 2

Corinthians. It reads:

> *Therefore we do not lose heart. Even though our*
> *outward man is perishing, yet the inward man*
> *is being renewed day by day. — 2 Corinthians*
> *4:16*

As we allow the Word of God to change and mold us, not a day goes by that our inner man does not look more and more like the Lord Jesus Himself.

2. God's glory is reflected to others.

As He is working on the inside of us, we reflect that same glory and majesty to all of those around us. This should give us a clearer picture when it comes to our role on the earth and why we are still here. It is the believer's privilege and responsibility to reflect the image of God to a world that desperately needs Him. We will look at our responsibility further in the final chapter of this book.

In review, let me give you some highlights of what the Holy Spirit is doing in us now.

- We have access to the Father anytime through the Spirit of God living on the inside of us.
- We are being changed daily into the image of Christ.
- As we change on the inside, we reflect Jesus to the world.

Let me conclude by saying again that God is able and willing to help us in any time of need as we approach His throne with confidence, believing that everything He is and possesses has been freely given to us - not for selfish gain but for the benefit of all. We benefit as we are transformed into Christ-likeness, and others benefit because they see who He is and what He will do through the window of our lives.

EXCEL

ex-cel \ik-'sel\ : *SURPASS, OUTDO : to be distinguishable by superiority: surpass others : FIRST CLASS*

Chapter 7

————— • —————

Excellent Advantage

————— • —————

In the previous chapters, we learned much about what Jesus did for us. Now, I want us to focus on the tools He freely gave us to use the moment we were born again. After His resurrection, Jesus gave us several tools, gifts, and graces to ensure the Church's continued success throughout all generations. There are many things the Lord has given His people because of His love for us, but for the sake of this study, we will only focus on those things that specifically were given as a result of the New Birth.

Let's start with one of the greatest, yet most underestimated, tools Jesus gave to His Church.

The Name of Jesus

One symbol of authority that He gave us was the name of Jesus. Jesus not only redeemed us, remitted our sin, and delivered us out of Satan's authority; He also gave us His authority when He gave us His name. Imagine that. He gave us the right to use the most powerful and influential name ever given. It's the same name whereby angels are still in awe and the same name that causes demons to tremble with fear.

It's the name above all names, the name of Jesus.

I heard a preacher once say that one of the hardest words for Christians to say is the name of Jesus. I have found that to be somewhat true. They do not mind saying Lord, Master, or even God, but even the name of Jesus can be very intimidating to those who do not realize that name has been given to them. Yet it has been given - not just for our possession but for our use.

We are to use His name in prayer.

"And in that day you will ask Me nothing. Most assuredly, I say to you, whatever you ask the Father in My name He will give you. Until now you have asked nothing in My name. Ask, and you will receive, that your joy may be full."
— John 16:23-24

We are to use His name when we are receiving those He has sent to us.

"Whoever receives one of these little children in My name receives Me; and whoever receives Me, receives not Me but Him who sent Me."
— Mark 9:37

We are to use His name to do miracles.

"For no one who works a miracle in My name can soon afterward speak evil of Me."
— Mark 9:39

We are to use His name to drive out demons.

"In My name they will cast out demons."
— Mark 16:17

One of the best illustrations that shows us how the name of Jesus is to be used is the concept of power of attorney. Many times when someone has to leave his country or state, he will have a trusted family member or friend to do business on his behalf. That individual must go before an attorney and have papers drawn up that will allow his trusted friend to provide representation in his absence. It is a tremendous responsibility on both parties. All this person has to do is to show the signed power of attorney and he can sign legal documents, take out loans, purchase property, and even make out a will, all in the name of the person who gave the authority. This is what Jesus did for us. He went before the high court of Heaven and signed the documents in His blood giving us authority to do business for Him while here on this planet. Glory to God! We need to stop running from the devil every time he rises up to threaten us. Instead, we must take the name of Jesus, stand up to him with the authority given to us, and defeat him every single time.

The next tool He has given us means more to Him than His own name.

The Word of God

For You have magnified Your word above all
Your name. — Psalm 138:2

A whole chapter later in this book is dedicated to God's Word. Because of that, I will not elaborate here except to say that the greatest gift God gave to humanity was His written Word.

The third tool is our source of power.

The Gifts of the Holy Spirit

For a list of the supernatural gifts that were given to us, we have to look in the book of 1 Corinthians.

But the manifestation of the Spirit is given to each one for the profit of all: For to one is given the word of wisdom through the Spirit, to another the word of knowledge through the same Spirit, to another faith by the same Spirit, to another gifts of healings by the same Spirit, to another the working of miracles, to another prophecy, to another discerning of spirits, to another different kinds of tongues, to another the interpretation of tongues. But one and the same Spirit works all these things, distributing to each one individually as He wills.
— 1 Corinthians 12:7-11

Many arguments have ensued over the validity of these gifts being in operation today. The truth is that they are still as valid today as they were 2000 years ago. As long as there is a church, there will be a need for the help of the Holy Spirit. Expect Him to work these gifts through you. Paul said we should desire spiritual gifts (1 Corinthians 14:1).

He also told us,

Now concerning spiritual gifts, brethren, I do not want you to be ignorant. — 1 Corinthians 12:1

For better clarity, I find it is easier to understand what the gifts are for if I understand what they do.

Think of them this way:

There are three gifts that know something (Revelation Gifts).

1. Discerning of Spirits
2. Word of Wisdom
3. Word of Knowledge

These gifts allow us to know what we could not normally know about a person or circumstance. They let us gain insight and give help, edification, and healing to others through the power of the Holy Spirit.

There are three gifts that say something (Speaking Gifts).

1. Tongues
2. Interpretation of Tongues
3. Prophecy

These gifts allow us to speak the will of God over a person, place, or situation. They take the limits off of us. When these gifts are in operation, we can pray or prophecy, proclaim or preach according to the will of God. When the Holy Spirit manifests Himself in these gifts, He gives what the Bible calls an unction, or a supernatural ability, to speak. The words that are spoken are for the building up of the Body of Christ.

There are three gifts that do something (Power Gifts).

1. Gifts of Healings
2. Faith
3. Working of Miracles

The power gifts are just that - gifts that manifest

the power of God through the miraculous. Every healing does not require the gifts of healings, but some do. For the most part, these demonstrations of the power of God are for a sign to the world, for they give witness to His awesome might.

Take Up Your Tools

Our job of winning the world requires as much power now as it did when the Church began many centuries ago. To gain a better understanding of God's idea of church, study the book of Acts in the New Testament. Religion may tell us that world evangelism can be done without the power of God in operation; however, it will never happen without the tools He provided. As the Church takes her rightful place using the name of Jesus, staying true to the Word, and flowing in the gifts of the Spirit, she will see the greatest move of God's Spirit this world has ever seen.

EXTOL
ex-tol \ik-'stol\ *: to praise highly : GLORIFY*

Chapter 8

———— • ————

Extolling With Rights

———— • ————

"...By This My Father Is Glorified..." — John 15:8

Prayer is where our position really gets its power. A prayerless Christian is at the same time a powerless Christian. Prayer is the tool God gave us for spiritual vitality. We are at our best when we are investing time with the Lord in prayer. Think about the unlimited truths that are a reality to the one who prays according to his or her position of right-standing with God.

- Miracles become a part of life.

- Present and future circumstances are always subject to change.

- The last word doesn't belong to the doctor, attorney, or even the court, and certainly not to the devil.

- "Never enough", "I can't", "it will never happen", and "impossible" are all words and phrases that mean very little anymore.

These are not just crazy ideas that some preacher came up with. If you will read a few chapters in any of the four gospels, you will see that there was something extraordinary about the life of Jesus. If you continue to read on through the book of Acts, you will see right away that the same could be said of the followers of Jesus. There was something about the ministry of Jesus that made people take notice. He spoke with an unprecedented authority like no prophet before Him had done. They watched as He raised the dead, healed the sick, quieted the storm, and fed the multitudes. They noticed the power that came after He would spend all night in prayer. It was His prayer life that made others want to pray. Of all the requests his disciples could have made after seeing Jesus minister to people, this is the one thing they requested of Him: They said, "Lord, teach us to pray." There was a unique correlation between the power of Jesus and the prayer life of Jesus. They cried out, "Lord, TEACH US TO PRAY!" And He did.

Let's look at a few scriptures that really bring out these truths. In the book of Luke, Jesus is teaching about prayer, and how to pray, when He tells the story about a man who, because of late arriving guests, was in need of some extra food. At midnight he realizes he must go to a friend of his and ask for bread. Jesus reveals to us that even though this man is a friend of his, it is because of the other man's shameless persistence that his friend gives him the bread. What a picture of effective prayer. Jesus is telling us that when we go to the Lord in prayer, we are supposed to go before the God of Heaven without shame but with persistence and boldness. For many, the idea of praying with such confidence, and with what could be perceived as arrogance and an ungodly audacity, seems like too much to conceive. But it doesn't offend God when we pray like this; it actually pleases Him. He wants His children to bear fruit, enjoy what He has provided for them, and never be governed again by Satan or any of his demons. The idea of being bold when we pray is not arrogance. It is, however, having an attitude of expectation and anticipation that what we have prayed for belongs to us - not because we decided out of the blue that it should be this way, but because the Word of God gives us the right to expect God to do what He said He would do.

Another remarkable lesson that Jesus demonstrated is in the book of John when He raised Lazarus from the dead. Let's look again at these scriptures.

> *Then they took away the stone from the place where the dead man was lying. And Jesus lifted up His eyes and said, "Father, I thank You that You have heard Me. And I know that You always hear Me, but because of the people who are standing by I said this, that they may believe that You sent Me." Now when He had said these things, He cried with a loud voice, "Lazarus, come forth!"* — John 11:41-43

Notice, again, the confidence that Jesus displays when telling the Father that He knows that He (the Father) always hears Him (Jesus). But notice this; both Martha and Mary had told Jesus if He had been there,

So GREAT A Salvation

their brother would not have died. They had more confidence in the prayers of Jesus than they had in their own. Of course we would have been the same way. After all, this was the Master. He was the Messiah. Please understand, though, that Jesus was working through a body back then. He became a man and purposed to be obedient to His Father and to allow the Holy Spirit to work through Him - a yielded vessel. He wants to work through His Body today. We are the body of Christ. Be confident in your relationship with the Father. He is the One who told us in the book of John,

> *"Most assuredly, I say to you, he who believes in Me, the works that I do he will do also; and greater works than these he will do, because I go to My Father. And whatever you ask in My name, that I will do, that the Father may be glorified in the Son. If you ask anything in My name, I will do it."*
> — *John 14:12-14*

Greater Works

Much has been taught on this verse of scripture. Many tell us that Jesus was talking about the entirety of the church body's work since inception, culminating in the "greater works". They say that all of the people who have been saved since Jesus died will together, through all of their works, equal a greater amount of works than He did. Others say Jesus was referring to how we would preach what He taught us which would lead to multitudes getting saved, and that this evangelism was the "greater works". Allow me to submit this proposition: Maybe He was telling us that when we allow Him to work through us to complete what He has asked us to do individually, then the "greater works" as Jesus called them would be done. I want you to think about something. For the first time in history, once a man was saved, or born again, the Spirit of God had the right to move inside of him. Since the fall of man when Adam and Eve sinned in the Garden of Eden, God could only come upon certain individuals and have them speak for Him or do works for Him. But because Jesus went back to the Father and sent the Holy Spirit to us, He was now able to literally move inside of us and make His home there. Jesus placed emphasis on this when He said, "Greater works than these will he do, because I go to my Father". The Spirit of God was no longer just coming upon man, but literally setting up His home in man. And when He moved in, all that belongs to Him came with Him. That's how greater works are possible. It's because of Him, not me. It's Him working through me. Greater works happen when I allow Him to do what He wants to do through me. Whether it is leading a person to Jesus or laying hands on the sick, or even doing something nice for someone in His name, whenever I yield to Him and allow Him to work through me, this is a greater work. In contrast to what every human being had ever experienced with God before Jesus, these greater works become a permanent and integral part of our daily lives, both individually and corporately. Pentecost was about more than power or prayer; it was an unprecedented paradigm shift from "God upon" to "God within" and from "God will someday" to "God will now". Why? Was it because the rules had changed? No, it was much more than that, for the makeup of man had changed.

His Greater Work in You

You may be called by God to be a business man. When you allow the Holy Spirit to lead you into all truth concerning your business, you are in fact doing a far greater work than you could imagine because you are allowing Him, who dwells on the inside of you, to lead, guide, and direct your path, and to empower you to do what you could not have done in your own strength. Now, because you are new, you can have a God-sized dream and God-sized resources to accomplish it; not because God sovereignly met you on the backside of a desert and spoke through a burning bush, but because you found an accurate picture of yourself within the pages of your Bible, and God shaped and formed you and said, "Walk in this new life I have given you - full of boldness and strength, armed with My Word, and empowered by My Spirit - and watch mountains be moved and see walls crumble before you as you move in the victory My blood has bought, bear much fruit, and bring glory to My Name."

It Shall Be Done

Let's look at another verse of scripture in John where Jesus tells us something even more remarkable.

"If you abide in Me, and My words abide in you, you will ask what you desire, and it shall be

done for you. By this My Father is glorified, that
you bear much fruit; so you will be My disciples."
— John 15:7-8

What a tremendous promise He has made to the ones who pray! Having a one on one relationship with Jesus, and allowing His Word to be the foundation for our lives causes us to exercise our authority as believers in the way God designed. Some people will take issue with this because they do not understand how much the Lord Jesus wants to manifest Himself to and through us.

What was the Lord teaching us in all of this? To pray? To heal? No, He was teaching us the greater truth of who our Father is. He did this because He understood that when we know the Father, we'll know how to pray. When we have knowledge of Him and what our relationship is to Him, we will pray as people having authority. We will pray as Jesus prayed. By this, our Father will be glorified because we bear much fruit.

EXALT

ex-alt \ig-zolt\ 1: to raise high :ELEVATE 2: to raise in rank, power or character

Chapter 9

---•---

Exalting The Word

---•---

In this chapter, I want to give you a summary of truths to use in your daily prayer and confession. Doing so will cause you to be exalted as God would have you to be. Remember, He is the One who said,

> *Therefore humble yourselves under the mighty hand of God, that He may exalt you in due time.*
> *— 1Peter 5:6*

God Wants To Exalt You

God has no problem whatsoever with us being exalted. He just does not want us exalting ourselves. He tells us to humble ourselves and let Him do the exalting. We need to know this because obedience to the Word will cause us to be exalted. Paul said, in 2 Corinthians 12, that he was exalted because of the revelation he had received. As in the case of Paul, that revelation will lift us above circumstances. It will exalt us above sickness and disease. It will cause us to be thrown beyond the typical and usual.

Humble yourself under His hand.

To humble oneself under the mighty hand of
God means to submit to Him. We submit to Him
when we submit to His Word. It does not matter how
much our flesh screams when someone does us
wrong or how much we are longing to do wrong
back to them, the Bible still tells us to do right. When
we choose to love someone who does not deserve
it, we are submitting to the Lord and to His Word. To
do so causes God to exalt us.

To humble oneself means to submit; it means to
yield. A humble person is one whose life is governed
by Bible-formed beliefs - one who has learned to
submit to those beliefs. Many of us think that in order
to become humble, something bad has to happen to
us. This is the world's way of understanding humility. The Bible's idea of humility is completely different. Humility means to retire from my way and yield
to another. Whenever I am retiring from the way I
think things should be and yielding to God's way of
doing things, I am being humble.

Humble yourself under His Word.

Humility is a choice we make on purpose and
with purpose. We do not become humble by accident.
It is possible to be humble in one area and prideful in
another. That's why the Word of God, and knowing
and applying the Word, is so important to the believer. God's Word is full of specific promises that belong
to us. However, as long as they stay unknown to us,
they stay untouched by us. These promises are sometimes prefaced with a command. An example of this

can be found in the book of Ephesians.

> *"Honor your father and mother," which is the first*
> *commandment with promise:"that it may be well*
> *with you and you may live long on the earth."*
> *— Ephesians 6:2-3*

Right away it is very clear that if we desire a long life and for everything to be well with us, then we will have to honor our parents. In other words, if we want the blessings of the good life, we will have to yield to and submit to God's Word regarding honor.

God Wants to Exalt His Word in Your Life

Jesus quoted the Old Covenant when He said,

> *"Heaven and earth will pass away, but My words*
> *will by no means pass away." — Mark 13:31*

In Matthew 4:4, Jesus also refers to this passage of Scripture:

> *That He might make you know that man shall*
> *not live by bread alone; but man lives by every*
> *word that proceeds from the mouth of the Lord.*
> *— Deuteronomy 8:3*

It is clear that the Word should have supreme place in our lives, and that we should look to it as our blueprint for everything we do.

In Psalm 119, we find a whole chapter that has been dedicated to the Word of God. By the way, it is also the longest chapter in the Bible and is located near to its center. Because of its placement and length, it is reasonable to suggest that it is very important in the eyes of God. Since it is so long, I will not go into dissecting the entire chapter. Instead, I will highlight some points of interest. Before I do, though, let me give some quick ground rules. Go ahead and get your Bible and turn there with me. Oh, and make sure you have a Bible that you can write in, mark up, and use. It's not going to do you any good sitting on the table looking at you. The Bible says of itself that it is a sword. But a sword does no good in battle sitting on your coffee table. It becomes a sword of the Spirit when it is planted in your heart through study and meditation and then comes out of your mouth in the form of confessions or declarations and in normal conversation. So think this way when you do the following exercise.

First, whenever you read the words *law, testimonies, precepts, ways, statutes, commandments*, and *judgments*, I want you to replace them with *Word* or *Word of God*. This will help in making it more real to you. Also, replace the personal pronouns and nouns the writer used to tell about himself with your name. For example, verse one and two would read:

Verse 1: *Blessed is <u>Douglas</u>, in the Way who walks in the Word of God.* Verse 2: *Blessed is <u>Douglas</u> who keeps the Word of God.* Look at verse 11: *God's Word has <u>Douglas</u> hidden in his heart that <u>Douglas</u> will not sin against God.* This is so good that I have to give you one more. In verse 46 a great promise reads, *<u>Douglas</u> will speak of God's Word also before kings, and will not be ashamed.* Now I want you to try it. Let's go to verse 105, and instead of my name, insert yours. It reads: *God's Word is a lamp to _____ feet, and a light to _____ path.* As you do this, you are speaking over yourself absolute truth. It will change your life.

You will find your true identity within the pages of the Word of God. I have said many times from the pulpit and from the pages you now hold in your hand that at the point of salvation, you were born again and became a new creature. You must learn from the Word of God what you are to act like, think like, talk like, and be like. You will discover truths like

- Who I am in Christ.

- Who Christ is in me.

- Where I am in relationship to my Heavenly Father.

- The authority that He has given to me.

So, I challenge you to take the following confessions and look up the scriptures for yourself. Be like Joshua and meditate on them daily. God instructed him concerning the place the Word was to have in his life. In Joshua, we read:

> *"This Book of the Law shall not depart from your mouth, but you shall mediate in it day and night, that you may observe to do according to all that is written in it. For then you will make your way prosperous, and then you will have good success." — Joshua 1:8*

Follow his example, speak the Word out loud, and boldly declare before kings who God is and what He has made you to be. It is then that, like Joshua, you will experience true prosperity and true success and you will move from good to great in your walk with God.

Scriptures to Meditate On

God has made me in His image (Genesis 1:27).

God has chosen me and calls me holy and dearly loved (Colossians 3:12).

God has loved me with an everlasting love (Jeremiah 31:3).

God has rescued me from the dominion of darkness and brought me into the kingdom of Christ (Colossians 1:13).

God has justified me so that I may have peace with Him (Romans 5:1).

God has reconciled me to Himself through Jesus Christ (Romans 5:11).

God has completely forgiven me (Colossians 1:13-14).

God has given me Christ's righteousness (Romans 5:19; 2 Corinthians 5:21).

God has justified me and will not condemn me (Romans 8:1, 31-34).

God sees me as blameless and holy (Colossians 1:22).

God has grafted me into His vine (Romans 11:17-18).

God has brought me near to Himself through the blood of Christ (Ephesians 2:13).

God has bought me with a price, and I belong to Him (1 Corinthians 6:19-20).

God gave me the right to become His child (John 1:12).

God has anointed and sealed me, and He makes me to stand firm in Christ (2 Corinthians 1:21-22).

Jesus calls me His friend (John 15:15).

Christ keeps me safe, so that the evil one cannot touch me (1 John 5:18).

Jesus is able to save me completely (Hebrews 7:25).

Jesus is making me holy (Hebrews 2:11).

Jesus has called me to bear fruit (John 15:5,8).

Christ allows me to approach God with freedom and confidence (Ephesians 3:12).

God's Spirit lives in me (1 Corinthians 3:16).

God has given me access to Himself by the Holy Spirit (Ephesians 2:18).

God is building me, as one of His living stones, into a spiritual house (1 Peter 2:5).

God has made me part of the Body of Christ and has given me specific spiritual gifts (1 Corinthians 12:27; Romans 12:6).

God has given me great and precious promises (2 Peter 1:4).

God will meet all my needs (Philippians 4:19).

God will give wisdom generously if I ask Him (James 1:5).

God provides mercy and grace to help in my time

of need (Hebrews 4:16).

God has given me a spirit of power, love, and self-discipline (2 Timothy 1:7).

God is able to keep me from falling (Jude 24).

God is strong in my weakness (2 Corinthians 12:9-10).

God has made me His ambassador (2 Corinthians 5:20).

God has made me a joint heir with Christ (Romans 8:17).

God is working all things together for the good of those who love Him (Romans 8:28).

God will complete the good work He has begun in me (Philippians 1:6).

I belong to God (1 Peter 2:9).

I am one of God's chosen people (1 Peter 2:9-10).

I cannot be separated from the love of God (Romans 8:35-39).

I am a new creation (2 Corinthians 5:17).

I am a child of the light and do not belong to the darkness (1 Thessalonians 5:5).

I am no longer a foreigner or an alien in God's house (Ephesians 2:19).

I am a citizen of Heaven (Philippians 3:20).

My life is hidden with Christ in God (Colossians 3:3).

I am a bondservant of Jesus Christ, pledged to

obeying Him (Romans 6:16-18).

My body is the temple of the Holy Spirit (1 Corinthians 3:16).

I am holy, and I share in God's heavenly calling (Hebrews 3:1).

When I confess my sins, God will forgive me and purify me from all unrighteousness (1 John 1:9).

I am made complete in Christ (Colossians 2:7).

I know that my work in the Lord is not in vain (1 Corinthians 15:58).

I am receiving a kingdom that cannot be shaken (Hebrews 12:28).

EXPERIENCE
ex-pe-ri-ence \ik-'spir-ē- ə n(t)s\ *1:to have experi-ence of :UNDERGO 2: to learn by experience-expe-rience religion : to undergo religious conversion*

Chapter 10

—————•—————

Experiencing The Unusual

—————•—————

God has always used words such as *beyond the usual, abundantly above, more than,* and *good* when describing His viewpoint of how we should live. Over time, our perception of His viewpoint has become watered down. Many have accepted and become satisfied with the mundane, the average, and even the mediocre. But in order to live an unusual, extraordinary, and abundant life, we must look at life from God's perspective. And we must follow His plan for us. We must go to our Maker to discover how we are to function at our maximum potential.

Divine Design

In the book of 1 Thessalonians, the Bible reads:

Now may the God of peace Himself sanctify you completely; and may your whole spirit, soul, and body be preserved blameless at the coming of our Lord Jesus Christ. — 1 Thessalonians 5:23

This verse of scripture reveals a lot to us about who we are. It tells us we are a three part being. We are a spirit, we have a soul, and we live in a body. It could be said like this: I contact the physical realm with my body; I contact the mental realm with my soul (mind, will, and emotions); I contact the spiritual realm with my spirit. Because of the nature of this book, we are going to primarily focus on the spirit realm.

The Bible actually has a lot to say about the spirit of a man. Sometimes, such as in the case of the book of Romans, the writer uses the term *spirit* in reference to the human spirit, the Holy Spirit, or both at the same time. In order to clearly understand the meaning of such passages, we must know which spirit the writer is referring to. We must also understand that when a person is born again, his or her spirit is re-created. Jesus made reference to that in John's gospel when He said,

> *"Most assuredly, I say to you, unless one is born of water and the Spirit, he cannot enter the kingdom of God. That which is born of the flesh is flesh, and that which is born of the Spirit is spirit. Do not marvel that I said to you, 'You must be born again'."*
> *— John 3:5-7*

Your spirit is the part of you that was saved. It is now up to you to renew your mind with the Word of God and to allow the Word to help you take care of that physical body. It works like this: As you read and meditate on the Bible, the Holy Spirit who lives in your spirit will illuminate truth to your mind. This truth illumination can be concerning any area where you need insight including business, finances, your job, career choices, parenting, or anything else you have to deal with. He will reveal the Word to you like never before and tell you things about the future when necessary. This is what it really means to be led by the Spirit. It allows God the Father to communicate to your spirit by the Holy Spirit thus leading you into all truth. Spiritual development in this area is a must for every believer in order to have a fruitful Christian life. A strong spirit full of the Word of God can weather all of life's storms. Let me give you some verses of scripture that bring out these truths.

The spirit of man is the lamp of the Lord, searching all the innermost parts of his being. — Proverbs 20:27 NAS

But there is a spirit in man, and the breath of the Almighty gives him understanding. — Job 32:8

The spirit of a man will sustain him in sickness, but who can bear a broken spirit. — Proverbs 18:14

For what man knows the things of a man except the spirit of the man which is in him? Even so no one knows the things of God except the Spirit of God. Now we have received, not the spirit of the world, but the Spirit who is from God, that we might know the things that have been freely given to us by God. — 1 Corinthians 2:11-12

"God is Spirit, and those who worship Him must worship in spirit and truth." — John 4:24

You see, once a person has been born again, God Himself literally moves into that person. Remember what I said to you earlier. When God moves in, all that belongs to Him moves in also. All that we will ever need for life and/or ministry is found in God inside us! We need to become God-on-the-inside minded.

Develop Your Spirit Man

Spiritual development, as stated earlier, is a must for all Christians. What I want to do now is give you the most practical ways to ensure you develop your spirit into a strong one.

1. Read and meditate on the Word every day.

Remember what God instructed Joshua to do.

"This Book of the Law shall not depart from your mouth, but you shall meditate in it day and night, that you may observe to do according to all that is written in it. For then you will make your way prosperous, and then you will have good success." — Joshua 1:8

This is vital to ensure true success in any and every area of your life. The Bible tells us that we are to diligently study and understand what it says and means. In the book of Timothy, the Bible tells us the following:

Be diligent to present yourself approved to God, a worker who does not need to be ashamed, rightly dividing the word of truth. — 2 Timothy 2:15

I love how this reads in the Living Bible. Notice what the last part of this verse says.

Work hard so God can say to you, "Well done."
Be a good workman, one who does not need to
be ashamed when God examines your work.
Know what His Word says and means.
— 2 Timothy 2:15 NLT (emphasis mine)

This is absolutely without a doubt the most important thing a Christian can do. The Word of God is the blueprint for how we are to live our lives. Our destiny, future, prosperity, health, and eternity are all found in God's Word. It is our prescription for all that ails us and our answer to all of life's problems. It will never be out-dated and will always be relevant. It is God speaking to us. It is a love letter from God to me and to you.

2. Daily invest time with the Lord through prayer and fellowship with His Spirit.

Years ago, the Holy Spirit showed me that any time I was with the Lord in prayer was an investment. We should view time and money the same way. We all do three things with our money; we invest it, we spend it, or we waste it. We do likewise with our time. We are either investing it, spending it, or wasting it. Any time with the Lord should be viewed as an investment. It's an investment that will bring the return of a strong spirit.

3. Pray in tongues every day.

The Bible tells us how to maintain our spirit man.

But you, beloved, building yourselves up on your most holy faith, praying in the Holy Spirit.
— Jude 20

I will pray with the spirit, and I will also pray with the understanding. I will sing with the spirit, and I will also sing with the understanding.
— 1 Corinthians 14:15

One of the greatest tragedies in the Western World today is the diminishing value this practice is given in our churches. I believe there is a direct correlation between what we have allowed to happen with our prayer language and the loss of power evident in the Church today. We have laid down a core value that Jesus gave to us. I want you to think about something. When precedent was being set and established for the Church at the time of her birth, what was the first thing that the Lord Jesus gave her? The first thing He gave was power; power that came in the form of the Holy Spirit. When the believers that day were baptized in the Holy Spirit and spoke with tongues, the Bible tells us they went out with this new authority and power, and thousands came to the Lord Jesus. The pattern or blueprint that was established then still holds true today.

In Jude 20, we read the words *"building yourselves up"*. If we are going to build ourselves up physically we will eat right and lift weights. Our bodies will grow in strength and muscle mass when a certain amount of resistance is applied. Our minds will grow and strengthen when we read and challenge ourselves with problem-solving. Likewise, the spirit man becomes strong and built up by praying in the Spirit. Actually, the phrase *"building yourselves up"* could be compared to charging a battery. Praying in the Holy Spirit charges your spirit.

Another huge benefit of praying in tongues daily is that it helps you to pray out not only your future but that of your family's as well. I know this may be unbelievable to some reading this, but let's look and see what the Bible has to say about this. Let's look at a verse of scripture in 1 Corinthians.

> *For he who speaks in a tongue does not speak to men but to God, for no one understands him; however, in the spirit he speaks mysteries.* *— 1 Corinthians 14:2*

In this verse, the word *speak* is not referring to a public service where someone may speak out in another language. In this type of public gathering, there would always be someone to interpret the message that was given in tongues. Either the one speaking in tongues can interpret or someone else in the room who operates in the gift of interpretation. We see this clearly taught in 1 Corinthians.

> *If anyone speaks in a tongue, let there be two or at the most three, each in turn, and let one interpret. But if there is no interpreter, let him keep silent in church, and let him speak to himself and to God. — 1 Corinthians 14:27-28*

Verse 2 says, *he who speaks... does not speak to men but to God.* When I am speaking to God, I am praying. So this verse could read *he who prays* because that is exactly what it is referring to. The phrase *no one understands him* is true. Usually the one praying, and anyone else in the room, does not understand what is being prayed. But, let's focus on the last part of this verse of scripture which says, *"in the spirit he speaks mysteries."*

A mystery is something unknown. It can be something that has to do with our past, present, or future. This verse of scripture, because of the way it is written and what it emphasizes, would also read this way:

> *For he who speaks* (prays) *in a tongue; in the spirit he speaks* (prays) *mysteries.*
> *— 1 Corinthians 14:2 (emphasis mine)*

Do you see this? Whenever I am praying in tongues, I am praying things that I have not yet seen. My future is a place I have not been, but thank God, I can go there in my prayer life. Think about it. Praying in tongues is a way to pray out the will of God for your future.

Several years ago, while in Bible School, I had an almost unbelievable experience with praying out my future. It was one of the most unusual and life changing moments with the Lord I have ever had. Every Tuesday morning, all of the students would gather together in the church auditorium for a time of prayer. I remember one Tuesday in particular, the Lord spoke to me in my heart to pray in the Spirit. After about 15 minutes of praying in tongues, the Lord gave me this interpretation:

> *Do not worry about what I have for you after graduation. I have already prepared the way.*

Stay faithful to me while you are here. You will be called to a church. There will already be a small group of people to start with. There are three buildings: a sanctuary, a house, and a life center. You will start out full time as well.

I remember going home that day, typing out what I had prayed out earlier, and saving it on my computer. And then I actually forgot all about it. The extraordinary thing is that everything I prayed out came to pass exactly the way the Holy Spirit prayed it through my spirit. It was after I had been at my new church for four months that I found what I had written on my computer. It was an amazing reminder to me of how God is involved with our future, and how we can pray and literally walk out what we have prayed in the spirit.

4. Find a church that believes the Bible.

This is one of the most important decisions a person can make. Please do not underestimate it. It is more important to be in the right church than it is to have the approval of others - even family and friends. Some of you right now need to follow the Lord and quit following people. If I were looking for a church home, I would want to know what they believed and why. You can find out what a church believes by asking questions.

Please understand that many churches will tell you they believe the whole Bible. And many even believe they do. I am not going to target or judge any particular group or church, for that is not my intention here. I simply want you, the reader, to be well-educated in looking for the right church. It is important for good spiritual health to be fed a healthy diet consisting of God's Word. The following criteria would be helpful to know when looking for a church home. Does the church you attend, or are considering attending, believe:

- The Bible, in its entirety, is God's inspired Word?

- Heaven and Hell are both real and literal?

- Salvation is for anyone who will call upon the Lord Jesus Christ and make Him Lord and Savior?

- Holy Spirit baptism is a gift to all for empowering the believer for good works?

- The gifts of the Spirit are still active in the believer's life?

- Healing has been provided for us in what Jesus did through His death, burial, and resurrection?

I am sure that to many this sounds basic and elementary. The truth is that we are living in an age where most of the church growth in this country is through transfer growth (one church losing people to another). Many of our church growth strategies are based on meeting people's emotional needs. While this is good and necessary to do, what is happening is that people are not having their spiritual needs met. Sometimes in order to meet a person's spiritual need, they will have to hear scriptures and teachings that they do not like when they first hear them. The only true hope for a person's emotions will always come through that person's spirit man. This is the reason it is vital to be in a church where the Word is preached and exalted and your whole family is fed.

5. Fast often.

Perhaps you have heard that Jesus never commanded us to fast, but He did expect us to. He said twice in the Sermon on the Mount, "when you fast" (Matthew 6:16-17).

A spiritual mentor of mine taught that a believer should fast and also live a fasted lifestyle. What he meant by this was that you should not overeat or succumb to every craving. You should be led by your spirit and not your appetite. A fast strengthens your spirit and keeps your body or flesh under subjection to your spirit. This allows God to really lead you by communing with your spirit. There is probably nothing that will supercharge your spirit faster or with more power than fasting will. Fasting does not change God, but it does change you.

6. Develop relationships with spiritual people.

I believe that I must first define what a spiritual person looks like. A friend of mine gives the best definition I have ever heard when he says that a spiritually mature person is one who allows the Word of God to govern what he or she thinks, says, and does. Spiritual people form beliefs from the Bible, and then live their lives according to those same beliefs. The Bible is very clear when it tells us:

He who walks with wise men will be wise, but

the companion of fools will be destroyed.
— Proverbs 13:20

Don't underestimate this point. One of the most critical decisions a person can make is the choice to surround himself with spiritual people. It is a mistake that will affect your destiny to have close friends or mentors who are not people of the Word or who lack integrity. I am not saying that you should not have friends that are lost. We all need to be around people we can influence for Jesus. What I am saying is to watch who you allow to influence you.

7. *Tithe and give offerings generously.*

Faith in a God who cannot be seen is the essence of a strong spirit. There is no better way to develop faith than committing your finances over to Him. I challenge you to follow the Lord in this. Finances are the only area in which God tells us to test Him.

> *"Bring all the tithes into the storehouse, that there may be food in My house, and* **try Me** *now in this," says the Lord of hosts, "If I will not open for you the windows of heaven and pour out for you such blessing that there will not be room enough to receive it." — Malachi 3:10 (emphasis mine)*

Tithe means a tenth. It is giving back to the Lord a tenth of all that He has given to you. The tithe belongs to the Lord and is supposed to be given at your local church where you attend and receive spiritual nourishment. But also know this: The tithe is the minimum. Under grace we are to give to the work of the Lord above and beyond the ten percent. One reason for this is that it is up to us to win the world to Jesus. He wants us to use our money, and even be strategic with our money, so that people will come to Him.

In summary, let me remind you of those seven areas that, if followed, will help you to develop your spirit man into what the Lord wants it to be. Before I do, let me add that this is not an exhaustive list. There are other points of obedience to cover, but these are a good place to start. You will never get so strong and mature that you outgrow these steps. As you grow, they will become permanent practice in your walk with God. They are:

1. Read and meditate on the Word every day.

2. Daily invest time with the Lord through prayer and fellowship with His Spirit.

3. Pray in tongues every day.

4. Find a church that believes the Bible.

5. Fast often.

6. Develop relationships with spiritual people.

7. Tithe and give offerings generously.

EXECUTE
ex-e-cute \'ek-sə-kyüt\ 1: to put into effect ; carry out ; PERFORM 5: to perform what is required to give validity to SYN to carry out the declared intent of another

Chapter 11

---•---

Executing What We Believe

---•---

In this final chapter, it is my goal to motivate and stir you, the reader, concerning your role in fulfilling the Great Commission. You and I now have a role in this because we have made Jesus our Savior and Lord. He has commissioned us; therefore, it is our responsibility to take this message to those around us and to the rest of the world. Jesus told us right before He left to go back to the Father that He wanted us to be actively involved in getting others born again and discipled. Let's look at two verses that bring out this truth. In the gospels of Matthew and Mark, He commands us by saying,

> *"Go into all the world and preach the gospel to every creature. He who believes and is baptized will be saved; but he who does not believe will be condemned." — Mark 16:15-16*

> *"All authority has been given to Me in Heaven and on Earth. Go therefore and make disciples of all the nations, baptizing them in the name of the Father and of the Son and of the Holy Spirit, teaching*

*them to observe all things that I have commanded
you." — Matthew 28:18-20*

We find many things in these two verses of scripture. However, there are three points I want to
address that are very important when it comes to exe-
cuting our salvation.

1. We, the Church (individuals in the church
and each local church that comprises the
Universal Church) are supposed to be actively involved in preaching the gospel to every
person on this planet.

2. We, the Church, corporately and individually, are supposed to be involved in personally discipling others.

3. The authority to go is backed by the
authority the Father gave to Jesus in Heaven
and on Earth. Please allow me to elaborate
on this point.

First, let's again look at the scripture found in the
book of Matthew.

*And Jesus came and spoke to them, saying, "All
authority has been given to Me in Heaven and on
Earth. Go therefore and make disciples of all the
nations, baptizing them in the name of the Father
and of the Son and of the Holy Spirit, teaching
them to observe all things that I have commanded
you; and lo, I am with you always, even to the end
of the age." Amen. — Matthew 28:18-20*

Imagine your boss coming to you one day and
telling you that he was sending you to another city to

do his business. Your assumption in agreeing to the assignment would be five-fold.

1. He (your boss) would pay all expenses.

2. You would be representing him and the organization as you go.

3. Every decision you make would be backed by his authority.

4. Your boss trusts you to go in his place and carry out all transactions to completion.

5. You would be expected to be accountable to your boss for your actions when you return.

Believe it or not, all of these points are found in these three verses. Jesus tells us to go and that He will always be with us (pay the expenses). He lets us know that we represent Him (teaching them to observe all things He taught us). Every decision is backed by Him (all authority is given to Him). He trusts us and releases us to do the work (go therefore). And we will be accountable to Him (to the end of the age).

It is clear that Jesus' intent is for the Church to bring others to Him. It is also clear that when the Church takes her place in this Great Commission, He will back her with all the authority that has been given to Him. Jesus received His authority from the Father; we receive our authority from Jesus. This means that no matter what obstacle is in front of us, be it financial, political, economical, or social, if we will use the authority He has given us, we will see the doors open for us to preach the Gospel.

Jesus gave us a world view in His last sermon before He left the earth. Sometimes it is easy to have a world view when it comes to the billions who need Jesus. What I want to do, however, is paint a picture of our view of our world. I am talking about the world we live in - the immediate world around us. The one where we get up every morning, drink our coffee, and read the newspaper. The one filled with neighbors we do not know, relatives we do not like, and churches on every corner. A world where there are millions of lost and backslidden people who desperately need the love of God and the power of salvation as much as the tribal leaders do in the jungles of Peru. I am speaking of my country, the United States of America.

I imagine years ago in Europe, the leaders of the churches were experiencing what we are experiencing now. Church attendance and giving were on a sharp decline across the continent. Oh sure, there were some churches growing, but this was mainly due to transfer growth, with little or no evangelism. The spiritual authorities were under a kind of deceptive lulling to sleep, and they lost their passion for souls. They never realized their complacency would someday throw their countries into a cold dark future without God. It is a darkness that many of the countries are still deeply in to this day. And sadly, the United States will be subjected to the same fate if the Church does not wake up and seek the wisdom of God concerning the harvest.

Without a strategy to be evangelistic, a person, or a church for that matter, will not be. Whatever you may call it; soul winning, evangelism, or witnessing, it does not really matter. What does matter, however, is that we all understand the mandate we have been given. We are responsible to lead those whom God places in our paths to the Lord Jesus. Let me ask a couple of questions. How many people do you speak with on a daily basis, and how often do you share your faith in Christ? We live in a world with people all around us who face a literal Hell, and their only hope is the message of salvation that we have. Will you hear the call?

God is calling you. He knows that one person can only do so much, but all He requires is that you do your part.

Do Your Part

We all have a part to play, or a role to fill, in reaching the world. These roles can be broken down into three categories; going, sending, and praying.

1. Going

We are perhaps most familiar with this one. We've already established its importance in Matthew 28 and Mark 16. We must go into every man's world whether that means going to the nearest Wal-Mart or to a remote rain forest. For some, going means becoming a full-time missionary in a foreign land. For others, it means taking short trips, but for all of us, it means sharing the Gospel with those around us.

2. Sending

Not all of us are called to give our lives to sharing the Gospel in a foreign land, but some are. Not all are called to have ministries that reach millions of people through media, but some are. And if they are to go, we are to send them. Paul said,

> *How then shall they call on Him in whom they have not believed? And how shall they believe in Him of whom they have not heard? And how shall they hear without a preacher? And how shall they preach unless they are sent? As it is written: "How beautiful are the feet of those who preach the gospel of peace, who bring glad tidings of good things." — Romans 10:14-15*

How do we send them? We send them by giving of our resources and, specifically, our finances. In the Gospel of John, Jesus says,

> *"Do you not say, 'There are still four months and then comes the harvest'? Behold, I say to you, lift up your eyes and look at the fields, for they are already white for harvest! And he who reaps receives wages, and gathers fruit for eternal life, that both he who sows and he who reaps may rejoice together." — John 4:34-35*

3. Praying

Some may go and some may send, but we all must pray. Jesus urged us to pray for laborers when he said,

> *"The harvest truly is great, but the laborers are few; therefore pray the Lord of the harvest to send*

out laborers into His harvest." — Luke 10:2

We can also pray that doors would be opened for the preaching of the Gospel (see Colossians 4:2-3) and for spiritual eyes to be opened so that people will understand the truth (Ephesians 1:16-19). As we exercise our authority in prayer, we can see entire nations become open to the Gospel. Then we can send those who are called to go. As we do, we will reap the greatest harvest of souls yet.

The greatest fulfillment you will ever know is not just that you experience salvation in its fullness but that you are able to share it with others. There is no greater joy this side of Heaven. If you want to be happy, and if you want to live a life of purpose, then you must take what you have and give it away. Jesus said,

> *"And as you go, preach, saying, 'The kingdom of heaven is at hand.' Heal the sick, cleanse the lepers, raise the dead, cast out demons. Freely you have received, freely give." — Matthew 10:7-8*

Most of us are familiar with John 3:16. It tells us that our Father loved the world so much that He gave His best; He gave His Son. It was the greatest gift He could give. It is the greatest gift we will ever receive. And it is the greatest gift we will ever give to others. The happiest people on Earth are those who have found His great salvation and have committed their lives to taking it to every corner of the world. Won't you make that commitment today?

Come to the Father

If you really want to turn your life around, walk in the truth, and experience all that the Father has provided for you, you must first accept Jesus as your Lord and Savior. The Bible says,

> *If you confess with your mouth the Lord Jesus and believe in your heart that God has raised Him from the dead, you will be saved.*
> *— Romans 10:9*

That simple step of faith on your part is what will open the door to this new life as a child of God. Your Heavenly Father has always loved you. He desires to pour out His goodness, His mercy and His grace on you. He wants a relationship with you, but the only way He can have it is if you accept Jesus.

Jesus said in John 14:6, "I am the way, the truth and the life. No one comes to the Father except by Me." Jesus is your way to eternal life, to Heaven, to true happiness, to lasting peace. You don't need to search anymore to find Him. If you are reading this book, I am certain He has found you. Won't you give your life to Him right now? Pray this prayer from your heart today.

> *Father God, I believe that You sent Your Son to die for me and that He rose again. I confess now that I am a sinner, and I need your love and forgiveness. Come into my heart. Forgive my sins. I receive your eternal life and righteousness now.*

Give me peace, joy, and all that You promised. Fill me with your Spirit. I will live my life to glorify You. In the name of Jesus, Amen.

If you prayed that prayer, the blood of Jesus has washed every sin away. You are brand new in Him. Your past is gone and you have a bright future full of promise and purpose ahead of you. You can talk to your Heavenly Father every day. You can begin your journey as a Christian. As of this moment, you are born again. You've been given a clean slate and a fresh start. Now, it is time to start living for Him and learning from Him.

Find a church if you don't have one. Tell them you have just been born again. You need to be baptized in water as a sign of your faith in Jesus Christ as your Savior, and you need to be around people who can help you grow in your walk with the Lord. God never intended for any of His children to be alone. You are part of His family now. You're my brother or sister in Christ, and I welcome you into the family of God. I love you, but most of all, He loves you. His love will forever change you. And I know for certain you will never be the same again.

Chapter Notes

Chapter 1

1. Toronto Star – http://www.commondreams.org/scriptfiles/
    views03/1229-09.htm
2. John and Elizabeth Sherrill, forward, *The Happiest People
    on Earth*, Steward Press, ©1975, *p. x.*

Chapter 3

1. Stephen Morin – http://www.tdcj.state.tx.us/stat/
    morinstephenlast.htm
2. Rick Warren, *The Purpose Driven Life*, Zondervan, ©2002.

Chapter 4

1. My definition.
2. E. W. Kenyon, *The Two Kinds of Righteousness*, Kenyon's
    Gospel Publishing Society, ©1965, p. 34.
3. My definition.
4. James Strong, *Strong's New Exhaustive
    Concordance of the Bible*, Nelson, ©1990, #4821.

If you would like to have Douglas Crumbly speak at your church or conference, you may contact him by calling 706-234-4923 or emailing at pdc@ccor.info.